PORTS AND LOGISTICS SCOPING STUDY IN CAREC COUNTRIES

MARCH 2021

Contents

Tables, Figures, and Boxes

TABLES

FIGURES

BOXES

Preface

This study was launched in October 2019. Consultants conducted two field trips: first to Uzbekistan, Azerbaijan, and Georgia in November 2019, and second to Pakistan and Kazakhstan in January 2020.

Presentation and discussion of the study at the Central Asia Regional Economic Cooperation (CAREC) Transport Sector Coordination Committee was planned to be held in Istanbul on March 2019 but was cancelled due to the coronavirus disease (COVID-19) pandemic. The report was then circulated for review among development partners and CAREC member countries in June and July 2020, and feedback was received up to October 2020.

The study is structured in three volumes: Volume I is an executive report with main findings and conclusions, Volume II provides a detailed description of main ports and shipping routes serving CAREC countries, and Volume III contains the main plans and projects for ports and logistics in CAREC countries. Volume I is available in print and digital versions, while Volumes II and III are only available in digital versions.

The authors of the study are Ignasi Ragas, ports and logistics expert and team leader; Adrian Sammons, port operations expert; and Davron Khodjaev, logistics institutional development expert.

Abbreviations

ADB	–	Asian Development Bank
AFG	–	Afghanistan
ASCO	–	Azerbaijan Caspian Shipping Company
AZE	–	Azerbaijan
BCP	–	border crossing points
BRI	–	Belt and Road Initiative
BTK	–	Baku–Tbilisi–Kars rail line
CAREC	–	Central Asia Regional Economic Cooperation Program
CIM	–	Contract of International Carriage of Goods by Rail
CIS	–	Commonwealth of Independent States
CMR	–	Contract for the International Carriage of Goods by Road
COTIF	–	Convention concerning International Carriage by Rail
CPMM	–	Corridor Performance Measurement and Monitoring
DMCs	–	developing member countries
EAEU	–	Eurasian Economic Union
EBRD	–	European Bank for Reconstruction and Development
ECO	–	Economic Cooperation Organization
EDB	–	Eurasian Development Bank
E&S	–	environmental and social
EU	–	European Union
FEU	–	forty-foot equivalent unit or 40' container
GEO	–	Georgia
GDP	–	gross domestic product
GR	–	Georgia Railways
ha	–	hectare
IMAR	–	Inner Mongolia Autonomous Region
IMO	–	International Maritime Organization
KAZ	–	Kazakhstan
KGZ	–	the Kyrgyz Republic
KTZ	–	Kazakh Railways
Km	–	kilometer
LPI	–	Logistics Performance Index (World Bank)
m2	–	square meter
MON	–	Mongolia
mt	–	million tonnes
mtpa	–	million tonnes per annum
OECD	–	Organization for Economic Co-operation and Development
OSJD	–	Organization for Co-operation between Railways
pa	–	per annum
PIFFA	–	Pakistan International Freight Forwarding Association
PR	–	Pakistan Railways
PRC	–	People's Republic of China
Ro/Ro	–	roll on-roll off
RZD	–	Russian Railways
SEZ	–	Special Economic Zone
SMGS	–	Agreement on International Railway Freight Communications
SOE	–	state-owned enterprise

SWD	–	speed with delay
SWOD	–	speed without delay
SWOT	–	Strengths, Weaknesses, Opportunities, and Threats
TAJ	–	Tajikistan
TEU	–	twenty-foot equivalent unit or 20' container
TIR	–	International Road Transports Convention
TITR	–	Trans-Caspian International Transport Route
TKM	–	Turkmenistan
TMTM	–	Russian acronym for TITR
Tn	–	ton
Tn*Km	–	tons per km
TRACECA	–	Transport Corridor Europe Caucasus Asia
TSCC	–	CAREC Transport Sector Coordination Committee
UNECE	–	United Nations Economic Commission for Europe
UNESCAP	–	United Nations Economic and Social Commission for Asia and the Pacific
UTLC-ERA	–	United Transport and Logistics Company – Eurasian Rail Alliance
UZB	–	Uzbekistan
XUAR	–	Xinjiang–Uygur Autonomous Region

Executive Summary

1.   Only three countries from the Central Asia Regional Economic Cooperation (CAREC) have seaports—Georgia, Pakistan, and the People's Republic of China (PRC). The other three—Azerbaijan (AZE), Kazakhstan (KAZ), and Turkmenistan (TKM)—have ports in the landlocked Caspian Sea. The majority of CAREC countries rely upon open-sea ports of other non-CAREC countries as conduits for most of their exports and imports. This makes CAREC landlocked countries highly dependent on third countries infrastructure and transport network capacity, significantly the Russian Federation, Turkey, and Iran. In addition, ports in other non-CAREC countries such as the Republic of Korea, India, or the United Arab Emirates (UAE) play a significant role in supply chains to and from landlocked CAREC countries.

2.   This scoping study analyzes seaports and multimodal corridors serving CAREC landlocked countries. The purpose is to provide sufficient background to ports and logistics developments in the region and identify areas and potential activities that will require cooperation among the Asian Development Bank's CAREC developing member countries (DMCs) and development partners within the framework of the CAREC Program. The novelty of this study is that it looks both within and beyond CAREC countries' perimeters, while most CAREC work so far, e.g., the Corridor Performance Measurement and Monitoring, focuses only on transport chains within it.

3.   Moving freight to, from, and across the CAREC region involves substantial challenges not only due to geography and poor infrastructure, but also to human-made barriers built along history. Not surprisingly, CAREC countries feature high logistics costs and low logistics performance index (LPI). Despite improvements in recent years, moving freight across borders in CAREC countries still requires too much time, cost, effort, and uncertainty.

4.   However, Central Asia is reviving its historic role as a trade corridor and is experiencing significant growth in transported volumes, in particular those triggered by the PRC–Europe trade. Current infrastructure plans in CAREC countries are expected to improve connectivity and efficiency but might not be sufficient to accommodate all future growth. Moreover, planning shortcomings and political interference may lead to unwise allocation of resources.

5.   Being at the crossroads between Asia and Europe, CAREC countries are involved in a complex framework of multilateral and bilateral agreements that have resulted in a dense web of transport corridors and trade facilitation initiatives with mixed success. The extension of the Transports Internationaux Routiers agreement to all CAREC countries and to most of their neighbors and trading partners is an opportunity that should not be watered down by day-to-day procedures at border crossing points. Despite some improvements, harmonization of technical standards and procedures and compliance are still unresolved issues.

6.   The predominance of rail in transport chains in many CAREC corridors is both a structural advantage, since rail is a more environment-friendly mode, and a risk as railways companies are still too rigid and unreliable public sector entities. Moreover, some public sector railways play many different roles and do not always provide a transparent and level playing field for the private sector. Containerized rail transport is well developed in transport chains from ports in the PRC or the Russian Federation, but much less developed in transport chains from Mediterranean, Black Sea, and Arabian Ocean seaports. Identification and removal of barriers and bottlenecks that prevent more containerization along these corridors would improve the efficiency of transport chains and widen the options of port access.

7.   Some institutional and governance issues have been identified in CAREC countries' port sectors. Though issues vary per country, shortcomings reduce the ability of ports to meet modern needs of port development and management. Some ports also feature aging infrastructure from legacy design and operational activities that result in low productivity, unresolved port–city issues and land accessibility gaps and bottlenecks. At the time

that port authorities are struggling to overcome these issues, some greenfield ports projects have been proposed, quite often driven by a supply-side strategy that could result in underuse of built capacity.

8.   Multimodal corridors from ports to landlocked CAREC countries have been clustered in six groups. A summary of the assessment of these corridors is provided below:

(i)   **Baltic Sea.** (Corresponding to CAREC corridors 1 and 6b, c). The corridor from Baltic Sea ports (notably Riga, St. Petersburg, Klaipeda, and Gdansk) benefits from seamless rail connectivity, cooperation between railways companies (United Transport and Logistics Company) and the Eurasian Economic Union. However, it is relatively little used because of long distance and imbalance of flows. Moreover, limited capacity at the Poland–Belarus rail border crossings remains an issue.

(ii)   **Mediterranean and Black Sea.** (Corresponding to CAREC corridors 2 and 6a). This is a multimodal corridor per nature since transport chains may involve ferrying across Black and Caspian seas. Caps to vessel size apply at both seas what has various implications on costs and standards of service. This explains that overland routes to avoid them are happening. This corridor is being actively promoted by stakeholders from Azerbaijan, Georgia, and Kazakhstan, as well as those from Turkey and Ukraine through the Trans-Caspian International Transport Route/TMTM partnership, which has ambitions to offer an alternative route for the PRC–Europe trades. The corridor has received substantial investment in infrastructure, e.g. Caspian ports, Baku–Tbilisi–Kars rail, East–West trans Caucasus corridor, though a few gaps and bottlenecks still exist both in rail and road. Container rail traffic from Black Sea and Mediterranean ports to Baku and beyond is growing but still at low levels.

(iii) **Arabian Sea-Iran.** (Corresponding to CAREC corridors 3a, b and 6a, b). Iran offers the shortest route from Arabian Sea ports into some landlocked Central Asia countries and used to be a busy route before sanctions. Bandar Abbas has frequent shipping connections with Jebel Ali in the United Arab Emirates that acts a global transhipment hub for global containerized freight. For its part new Chabahar port is developing as a conduit for Indian trade to Afghanistan (AFG) benefitting from lesser restrictions. International containerized rail along the North–South corridor is hampered at present because of a still unresolved gap to link with Azerbaijan rail network and inadequate facilities for transhipment at Turkmenistan border.

(iv)   **Arabian Sea-Pakistan**. (Corresponding to CAREC corridors 5 and 6). Despite the presence of major international players and good capabilities, Pakistan logistics sector is underperforming. This is the cumulative effect of infrastructure obsolescence (e.g., in rail and road sectors), strong inertias at all levels that delay reforms, security issues, among other. Though Karachi is still by large the major gateway port for AFG, and that the new Gwadar port ambitions to become a second one, there is a risk that a growing share of this trade shifts to Iranian ports. A new Government Logistics Policy, the implementation of International Road Transports Convention and stability in AFG offers some opportunities for ports in Pakistan increasing their role as gateways into Central Asia.

(v)   **Pacific-Trans-PRC.** (Corresponding to CAREC corridors 1, 2 and 5). This corridor is the most relevant for Central Asia trades mainly with Lianyungang and Tianjin seaports. The corridor features well developed and reliable containerized rail connections that benefits form improved transhipment infrastructure at KAZ–PRC border crossings. The picture is less bright for the Mongolia/PRC corridor that is somehow peripheric to the PRC–Europe so-called land bridge. Despite improved rail transhipment infrastructure, long times are still required to go through border crossing points (BCPs). Also infrastructure gaps, e.g. rail linking Uzbekistan (UZB)–the Kyrgyz Republic (KGZ)–the PRC, and bottlenecks on mountain roads connecting KGZ/PRC and Tajikistan/PRC reduce the options of these countries for alternative and more direct routes. PRC–Central Asia corridor faces two main risks: one is the long-term durability of subsidies to rail applied by Chinese authorities; a second one is that focus on PRC–Europe block trains may impact negatively at flows to and from Central Asian countries, e.g., capacity shortages, higher transport fares, less priority when allocating rail slots, etc.

(vi)   **Pacific-Trans Siberia**. (Corresponding to CAREC corridors 3 and 4). On average this is a less relevant corridor than the previous but still vital for some Central Asia countries (e.g., UZB) and provides reliable and efficient connection to Korean (Busan) and Japanese seaports. The corridor offers robust rail infrastructure and seamless connectivity, benefiting from same rail standards but also faces similar risk, i.e., that growing East–West (Europe) traffic crowds out traffic bound to Central Asia. Because of distances, this corridor is not a workable option for road transport into Central Asia

9.   This scoping study also includes an assessment of CAREC plans and projects in ports and logistics for the past years. During 2014–2019, DMCs presented plans and projects in transport and logistics at CAREC Transport Sector Coordination Committee amounting up to $44.2 billion. The split in terms of value is: 51% were road projects, 38% rail projects, 8% ports, and 3% logistics projects. Interestingly the major port project presented is still on hold and logistics projects seem not to have materialized either.

10.   From the analysis of past experience in CAREC countries and discussions with some development partners some issues in ports and logistics planning and policy have been identified: (i) protection of internal markets driving transport policy, (ii) poor planning process and practice; (iii) inappropriate skills in government planning offices, (iv) hesitancy and inconsistency in the application of public–private partnership and user pays mechanisms, and (v) logistics projects non-aligned with logistics needs.

11.   A series of recommendations are drawn from the analysis of ports, multimodal corridors, and experience in planning and projects. These recommendations are structured in four pillars and sketched below.

Pillar I. Institutional

1   Open national transport markets.
2   Continue efforts to streamline border crossings.
3   Harmonize standards and regulations in transport and logistics.
4   Improve quality of regulations.
5   Continue reforming railways.

Pillar II. Infrastructure

1   Align logistics planning with logistics needs.
2   Improve port connectivity.
3   Promote international standards in logistics infrastructure.
4   Improve knowledge about CAREC freight flows.
5   Promote good practice in planning including Environmental and Social safeguards.

Pillar III. Operations

1   Promote efficient and competitive intermodal solutions.
2   Increase predictability and reliability.
3   Progress toward digitalization and smart ports and logistics.
4   Promote the environmental dimension in ports and logistics.

Pillar IV. Capabilities and skills

1   Strengthen business and professional ecosystems.
2   Promote qualifications and skills in logistics.

12.   The report concludes with a suggestion of next steps under the CAREC framework for the short-medium term. The proposed actions avoid repeating what is already proposed in CAREC Transport Strategy 2030 but add complementary fields. These proposed actions are the following:

(i)   Cooperation partnerships with regional organizations involving non-CAREC transit countries.
(ii)   Knowledge sharing on best practice in ports and logistics infrastructure
(iii) Identification of opportunities for multimodal corridors
(iv)   Complement corridor performance measurement and monitoring with multimodal logistics
(v)   Exchanges with national logistics organizations
(vi)   Prepare country, port, and/or corridor focused reports

1. Introduction

1.1. Objective

This scoping study analyzes sea ports and multimodal corridors serving the landlocked countries of the Central Asia Regional Economic Corridor (CAREC). The ultimate objective as defined by the terms of reference is to provide sufficient background to ports and logistics developments and identify those areas and activities which will require close cooperation among CAREC developing member countries (DMCs) and development partners within the framework of the CAREC Program.

1.2. Pertinence of a Ports and Logistics Scoping Study

Cross-border transport and logistics is included as one of the key pillars of the CAREC Transport Strategy 2030. Intense research has been made under the framework of CAREC on improving capacity, efficiency, and safety of the defined CAREC corridors, not to mention other aspects such as financial sustainability and environmental and social impacts.

CAREC countries rely upon open-sea ports of third-party countries outside of their borders as conduits for their exports and imports. These open-sea ports are located mostly in non-CAREC countries and act as international oceanic trade nodes to connect CAREC freight moving on cross border railways, highways, inland sea shipping, and on river and canal barges.

CAREC landlocked countries are highly dependent on the neighboring countries' infrastructure and transport network capacity to transport their traded goods to and from the nearest ports. Transport infrastructure impacts on trade passing through transit countries and thus the ability from landlocked countries to compete in global markets. The relative impact of the weak infrastructure of its neighbors has a particularly negative impact on those landlocked countries, which mainly export primary commodities with low value-to-cost ratios rather than high-value products or service (Carrere & Grigoriou 2011).

These reasons underpin the pertinence of providing an integrated view of ports and logistics corridors serving CAREC countries and explore

Container train approaching Altynkol Station in Khorgas, Kazakhstan.

complementarity, but also gaps, in the pillars and in the working lines envisaged in CAREC Transport Strategy 2030.

1.3.   Timing and Perspective

This project was launched in the fourth quarter of 2019. Field visits to Uzbekistan, Azerbaijan, and Georgia were made in 2019. Visits to Kazakhstan and Pakistan were made in the first quarter of 2020. At the same time contacts and videoconferences with other CAREC countries stakeholders were made. Accordingly, most of data and qualitative information used for this report was received just before coronavirus disease (COVID-19) pandemic.

Though the impact of the pandemic was felt acutely across the region in 2020 at the time of writing this report, freight flows and logistics were relatively less affected that other activities and industries such as aviation, personal mobility, tourism, and accommodation, among others.

Despite the uncertain times when this report has been produced, the authors consider that (i) this scoping study focuses on long-term trends that are most likely to remain in place after the pandemic, and (ii) it is too early to appropriately ascertain the long-term full impacts of the pandemic (Wilding 2020).

1.4.   Structure of the Study

This study has been structured in three volumes:

Volume I is an executive report that provides the main findings and conclusions of the study.

Volume II provides a detailed description of main ports and shipping routes serving CAREC countries.

Volume III provides a detailed list of main national plans and projects in ports and logistics in CAREC countries in recent years.

2. Corridors Linking Landlocked CAREC Countries to Seaports

2.1. CAREC Countries' Access to Seaports

Landlocked CAREC countries include Afghanistan, Azerbaijan, Kazakhstan, the Kyrgyz Republic, Mongolia, Tajikistan, Turkmenistan, and Uzbekistan. Six of the 11 CAREC countries host seaports though three of these countries (Azerbaijan, Kazakhstan, and Turkmenistan) host ports on the landlocked Caspian Sea. Georgia has ports on the Black Sea that feed into the Mediterranean Sea through the Bosphorus Strait. Pakistan and the People's Republic of China (PRC) are the only two CAREC countries that host open-sea ports capable of serving large bulk and container ships. The PRC has the higher capacity port infrastructure that attracts the widest range of shipping services.

Before considering the significance of open-sea ports in third party countries it is important to note that international trade through seaports in Pakistan and the PRC cannot offer a total solution to the CAREC region as a whole. This is because the varied locations of traded goods to and from CAREC countries will dictate use of third-party ports and various modalities. These factors emphasize the importance of international seaports and transport corridors located in third party countries to CAREC nations trade activity.

2.2. Ports and Hinterlands

In CAREC landlocked countries, production and consumption centers are mostly located more than 800 kilometers (km) away from the closest seaport. This equates to 2 or more days' travel time. In some CAREC countries the distances are even greater, ranging between 1,500km and 6,000km.

In an ideal world, landlocked countries would use closer ports as default gateways. However port hinterlands are defined not only by distance but by a series of factors such as the main origin and destination of cargoes, the maritime connectivity of ports, the existence of consolidated, and reliable multimodal transport, availability of backhaul cargoes, and institutional aspects (e.g., ease to cross borders, security, trade and transport agreements). These kind of factors explain that though Iran and Pakistan ports are closer to some Central Asian countries such as Tajikistan, Turkmenistan or Uzbekistan (on the range of 2,000 km) they are less used than other ports located much further away (up to 4,000 and 5,000 km) in the Pacific or the Baltic. Port hinterlands also depend on the competitiveness of direct land transport vis-à-vis feedering. As an example, some cargoes to Georgia may

Table 1: CAREC Countries with Sea Port Access

CAREC Country	Landlocked	Sea Port Access	Range to Nearest Sea Port (kilometer)	Mode of Access to Nearest Sea Port
Afghanistan	Yes	Nil	1,200–1,600	Road
Azerbaijan	Yes	Caspian	800	Rail–Road–Canal
Georgia	No	Black Sea		
Kazakhstan	Yes	Caspian	3,000	Road–Rail–Canal
Kyrgyz Republic	Yes	Nil	4,500–5,200	Rail–Road
Mongolia	Yes	Nil	1,700–6,000	Rail–Road
Pakistan	No	Arabian Sea		
People's Republic of China	No	Pacific		
Tajikistan	Yes	Nil	1,500–2,500	Rail–Road
Turkmenistan	Yes	Caspian	1,600	Rail–Road–Canal
Uzbekistan	Yes	Nil	2,000–1,800	Rail–Road

CAREC = Central Asia Regional Economic Cooperation.

Source: UNCTAD 2014 and consultants' calculations.

use land transport from a Turkish port instead of using feeder services across the Black Sea.[1]

In all cases the distance to a seaport not only adds costs and travel time, but also has consequences at the operational level. Long transit times imply extended period financing traded goods and fewer front-haul trips over a given period and often facing costly and long empty return journeys. The reduction in transport productivity results in lesser return on investment for the transport operators in vehicles or infrastructure. Such a sequence dissuades investment in transport capital equipment and may lead to low quality of services provided by old, less reliable and less carbon-friendly transport vehicles.

Few landlocked CAREC countries can be described as captive hinterlands of particular ports. The closest to that notion would be Azerbaijan for Georgian ports and Afghanistan for Pakistani ports. However, in both cases

their markets are also contested by ports in Turkey, the Russian Federation, or Iran. The most part Central Asia is a contested hinterland of several ports located east, west, and south of their landmass. Thus the interest manifested by third party countries in particular the PRC, but also the Russian Federation, and to lesser extent the European Union (EU), India, or Turkey in the development of new ports, intermodal transport corridors, and trade and transport agreements to facilitate access to this vast hinterland.

In this study, ports and corridors linking landlocked CAREC countries have been clustered into six groups. Some of these corridors extend into the open-sea ports through non-CAREC countries, notably the Russian Federation, Iran, and Turkey. For each corridor the equivalence into CAREC corridors is mentioned. The assessment of ports, shipping, and multimodal corridors in this report has been structured according to these corridors which are illustrated in figure 1.

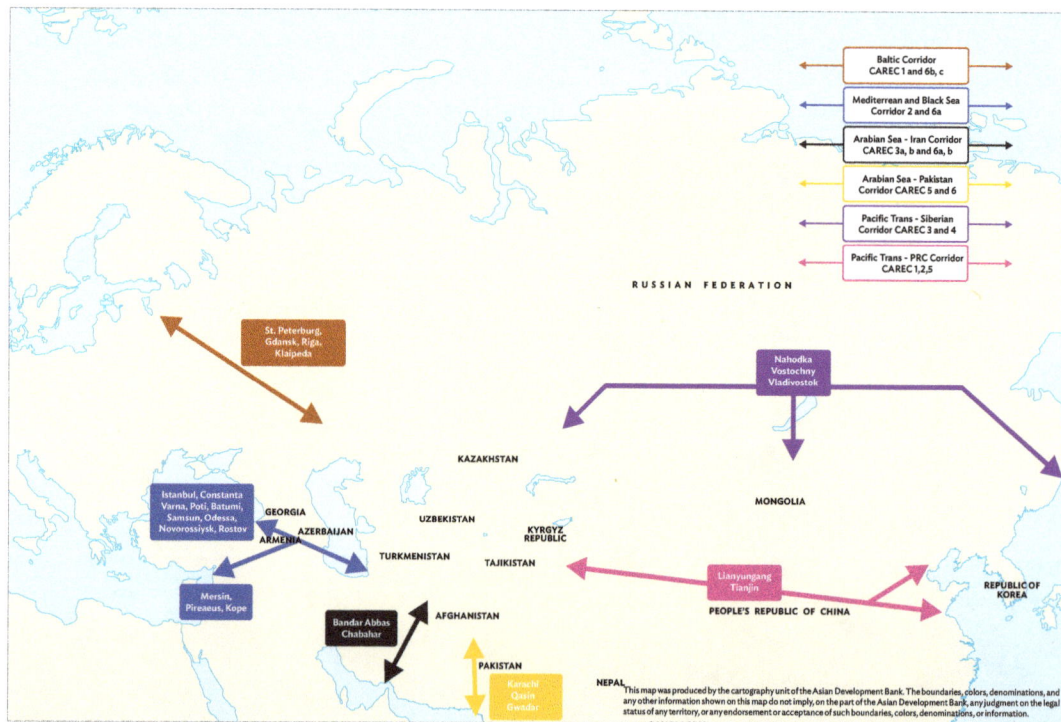

Figure 1: Illustration of Corridors from Landlocked Countries to Open Sea Ports

CAREC = Central Asia Regional Economic Cooperation, PRC = People's Republic of China, RUS = Russian Federation, TUR = Turkey, UKR = Ukraine.

Source: Consultants' team.

---

[1]   The consultants found evidence of these practices. When asking quotes for shipments from Europe to Georgia to a major shipping company that operates a container terminal in a Georgian port, some of those shipments appeared to be routed to a Turkish port and then moved by road to Georgia.

A snapshot of main ports and shipping connections in these corridors is sketched in the following sections in this chapter. A detailed description of main ports and shipping routes serving all these corridors can be found in Volume II of this report.

2.3. Baltic Corridor (CAREC 1 and 6b, c)

- CAREC countries most likely to use the Baltic Corridor are Kazakhstan, the Kyrgyz Republic, Tajikistan, and Uzbekistan.
- Major ports at the head of this corridor are Riga (Latvia), Saint Petersburg (Russian Federation), Gdynia/ Gdansk (Poland), Klaipeda (Lithuania) and, to lesser extent, Kotka (Finland) and Tallinn (Estonia). Some cargo may also come directly into CAREC countries from other major ports such as Hamburg, Rotterdam, or Antwerp.
- Corridor connections to CAREC runs across the Russian Federation, Belarus, and some EU countries such as Poland and the Baltic Republics.
- Main international container shipping connections from Baltic ports are:
  - East Asia, the PRC and Southeast Asia via Colombo and Singapore.

- Feeder services from major hub ports in Europe's North-Atlantic rim such as Hamburg, Rotterdam, or Antwerp.
- Ferry services offering Ro/Ro and passenger connectivity with other Baltic and Scandinavian ports.

2.4. Mediterranean and Black Sea Corridor (CAREC 2 and 6a)

- CAREC Countries most likely to use this corridor are Georgia, Azerbaijan, Turkmenistan, Kazakhstan, Uzbekistan, the Kyrgyz Republic, and Tajikistan.
- Major ports at the head of this corridor are Poti and Batumi in Georgia, Mersin and Istanbul in Turkey, Constanta in Romania, Varna in Bulgaria, Novorossiysk and Rostov in the Russian Federation, and Odessa in Ukraine.
- Corridor connections to CAREC crosses the Black Sea from third party ports to Georgia and Azerbaijan and then either sail across the Caspian Sea or circumvent it by land across the Russian Federation to reach Central Asia. Some cargoes, typically out of gauge, are shipped from the Black Sea to the Caspian along the Volga–Don inland canal system.

Figure 2: Main Baltic Seaports Large-Scale Map

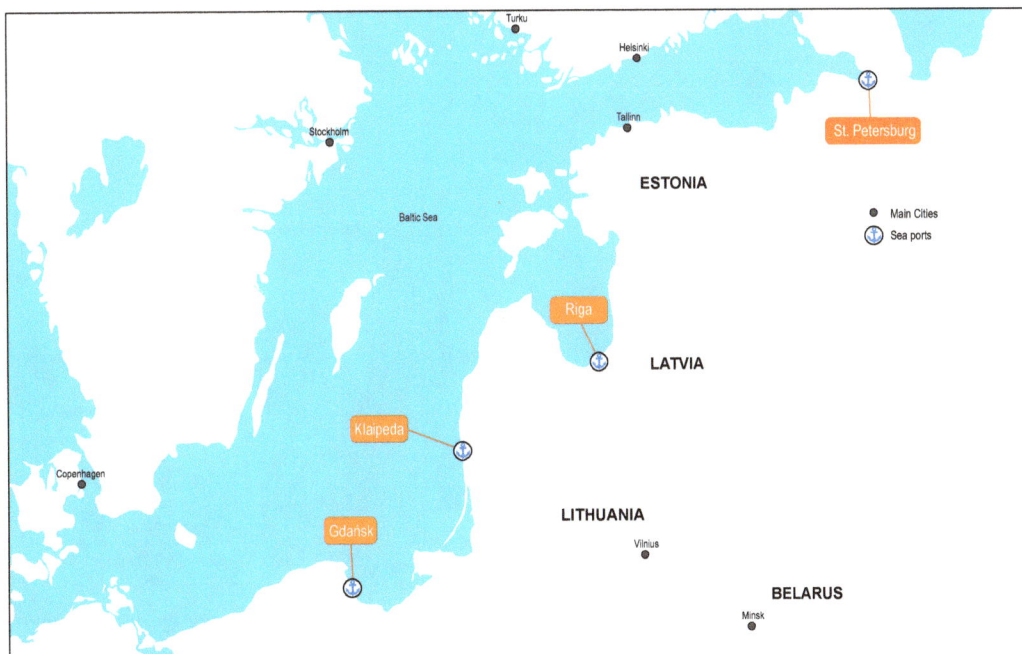

Source: Netpas navigation service and consultants.

Figure 3: Main Mediterranean Sea Ports Large-Scale Map

Source: Netpas navigation service and consultants.

Figure 4: Main Black Sea Ports Large-Scale Map

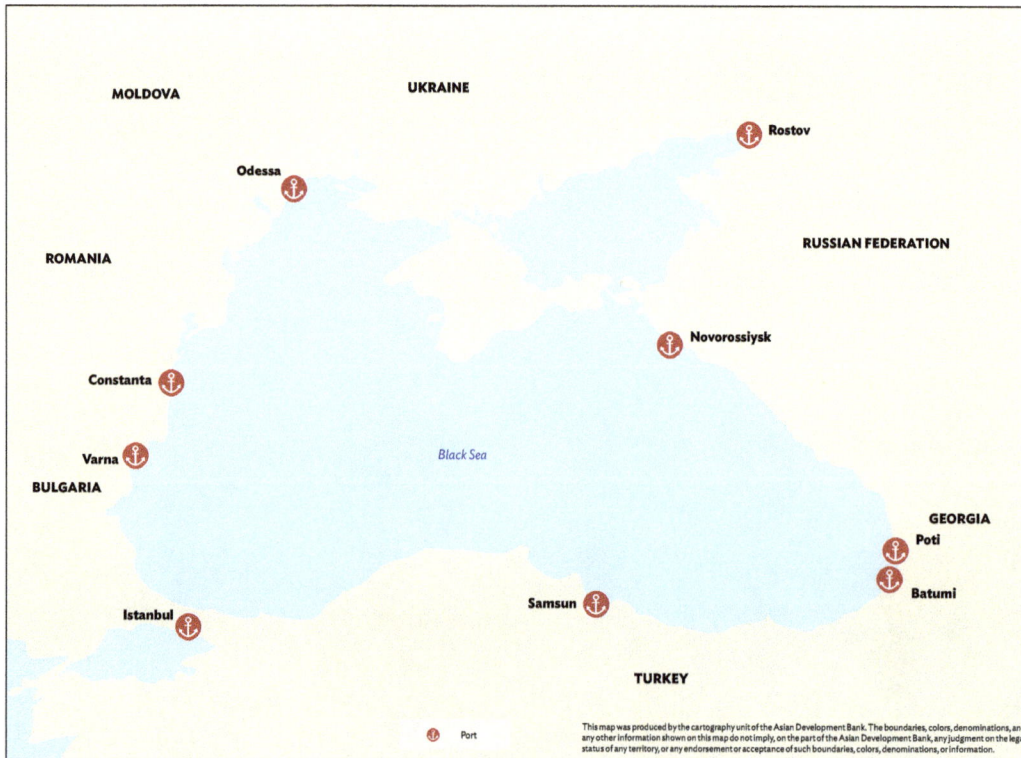

Source: Netpas navigation service and consultants.

Figure 5: Caspian Sea Ports Large-Scale Map

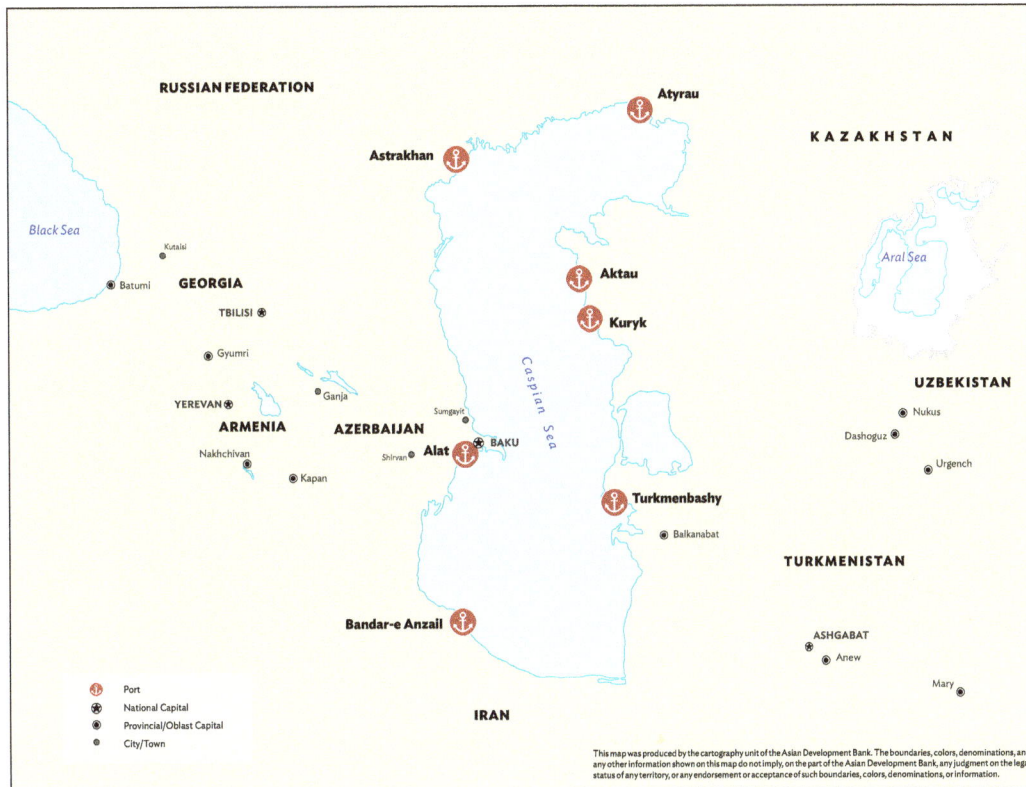

Source: www.netpas.net and consultants.

- Main Caspian Sea ports are Alat in Azerbaijan, Astrakhan in the Russian Federation, Aktau and Kuryk in Kazakhstan, Turkmenbashi in Turkmenistan and Bandar Anzali in Iran.
- The Black Sea connects through the Bosphorus Strait to the Mediterranean Sea and thereafter to the Atlantic Ocean through the Straits of Gibraltar and through the Suez Canal to the Red Sea and Indian Ocean.
- International container shipping connections from Black Sea ports includes:
  - Georgia's ports of Batumi and Poti connect with Constanta port in Romania, Varna in Bulgaria and the Russian Federation's port of Novorossiysk and Chornomorsk in Ukraine.
  - Azov Sea ports connect with the Volga Don and act as hubs for the northern Baltic ports.
  - Ukraine's ports of Nikolayev, Odessa, İlichevsk compete with the Russian Federation for scheduled shipping services and feeder routes in the Black sea that connect with Batumi and Poti.

- Romania's ports of Constanta and Bulgaria's port of Varna are key links with European overland corridors inking with Black Sea shipping services to bordering ports in most other countries.
- Turkey's ports of Samsun and Istanbul provide major transhipment connections for intercontinental shipping to all other world ports.

2.5. Arabian Sea - Iran Corridor (CAREC 3A, B and 6A, B)

- CAREC Countries most likely to use this corridor are Afghanistan, Azerbaijan, Turkmenistan, and Uzbekistan.
- Major ports at the head of the corridor are Bandar Abbas and, to lesser extent, Chabahar port.
- Corridor connections to CAREC crosses Iran and then into Afghanistan or Turkmenistan.
- The CAREC corridors identify ports in Iran for connection through to Afghanistan and into

Figure 6: Main Arabian Sea Ports Large-Scale Map

Source: Netpas navigation service and consultants.

bordering states including the PRC, Uzbekistan, the Kyrgyz Republic, and Tajikistan. Iranian ports in the Persian Gulf are also an important connecting waterway hosting some of the world's largest transhipment ports by volume, including Jebel Ali in the UAE, which provides global transhipment connections.

- International container shipping connections from Iranian ports include
  - Jebel Ali — Bandar Abbas (Jebel Ali port acting as transhipment hub for global containerised freight movements to/from the CAREC region).
  - Indian ports to Chabahar at irregular schedules that connect CAREC to India merchandise trade activity and transhipment to and from global ports through Indian ports. Chabahar is still in development.

2.6. Arabian Sea - Pakistan Corridor (CAREC 5 and 6)

- CAREC Countries most likely to use it are Afghanistan and to lesser extent Tajikistan, Uzbekistan, and the Kyrgyz Republic.
- Major ports at the head of the corridor are Karachi ports, Bin Qasim and Gwadar.

- Corridor connections to CAREC crosses Pakistan then into Afghanistan at border crossing points most notably Torkham and Chaman. Thereafter into other Central Asia either across Afghanistan or the PRC.
- International container shipping connections from Pakistani ports include:
  - Karachi and Bin Qasim as gateway ports for global containerised freight movements to and from the CAREC region that connect to global transhipment ports at Colombo, Singapore, and Jebel Ali.
  - Chinese ports to Gwadar at irregular schedules that connect CAREC to Chinese merchandise trade activity and transhipment to and from global ports through Chinese ports. Gwadar is still in development.

2.7. Pacific Trans-PRC Corridor (CAREC 1, 2, 5)

- CAREC Countries most likely to use it are Mongolia, Kazakhstan, Uzbekistan, Turkmenistan, Tajikistan, Azerbaijan, the Kyrgyz Republic, and Georgia. This corridor also conforms the PRC–Europe "Land Bridge."

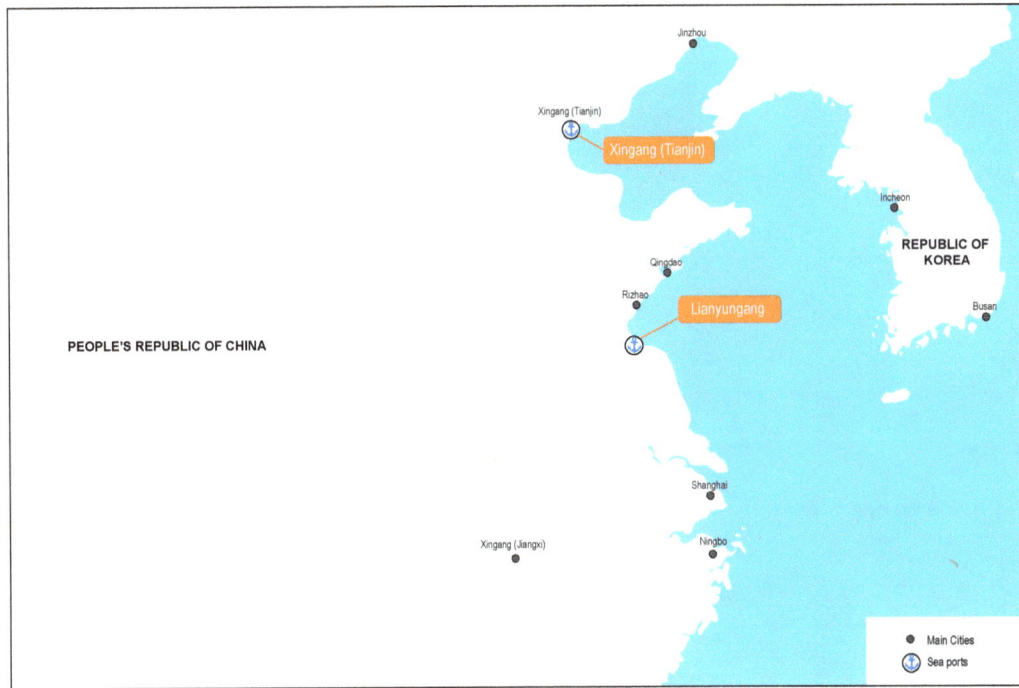

Figure 7: Main Pacific Ocean Ports North East Asia Large-Scale Map

Source: Netpas navigation service and consultants.

- Major ports at the head of the corridor are Shanghai, Lianyungang, Tianjin–Xingang, and other major Chinese container terminal ports.
- Corridor connections to CAREC crosses continental PRC from recognized rail hubs at Lianyungang and into Kazakhstan. Thereafter into other Central Asia countries through Uzbekistan and other bordering states.
- International container shipping connections from Chinese ports include:
  - Lianyungang, Shanghai, and Tianjin–Xingang that connect with for global containerised freight movements to and from the CAREC region with global gateway ports in Southeast Asia, United State west coast, and Europe.
  - Chinese ports also attract regular shipping services that connect to Western Europe for Chinese exports that may link through Mediterranean and Baltic ports that connect to CAREC countries.

- Chinese merchandise trade may also be routed via Pakistan and Iran for connection to Afghanistan and, to much lesser extent, other CAREC countries.

2.8.   Pacific Trans-Siberia Corridor (CAREC 3, 4)

- CAREC Countries most likely to use this corridor are Mongolia, Kazakhstan, and Uzbekistan.
- Major ports at the head of the corridor are Vostochny, Nakhodka, and Vladivostok.
- Corridor connections to CAREC crosses the Russian Federation into Mongolia or into Kazakhstan and thereafter into other Central Asia countries.
- The majority of shipping connections for containerized cargoes through these Russian ports are with Korean, Japanese, and Far East Pacific coast ports in the PRC and Taipei,China.

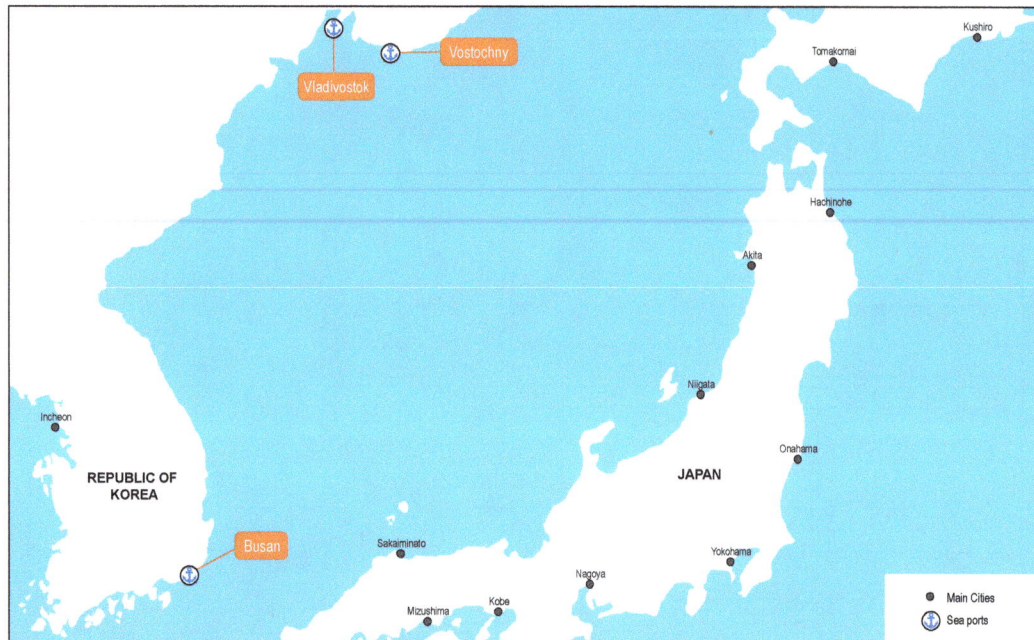

Figure 8: Pacific Ocean Ports North Asia and Russian Federation Large-Scale Map

Source: Netpas navigation service and Consultants.

Table 2: Summary of Main Ports Serving CAREC Countries

	Port Name	Port Capacity (mtpa)	Combined Throughput (mt)	Container capacity ('000 TEU pa)	Containerized Throughput ('000 TEU)
Baltic Sea	GDANSK	60.0	52.0	3,250.0	1,948.9
	RIGA	63.0	32.8	1,100.0	467.0
	KLAIPEDA	65.0	46.3	1,200.0	703.0
	ST PETERSBURG	80.0	59.2	4,200.0	2,097.0
Med. Sea	ISTANBUL	205.0	108.0	16.000,0	8,500.0
	MERSIN	48.2	32.5	2,600.0	1,960.0
	PIRAEUS	93.8	50.9	7,200.0	5,650.0
	KOPER	37.0	24.0	1,300.0	988.0
Black Sea	SAMSUN	23.0	12.2	125.0	67.0
	VARNA	15.0	9.5	300.0	139.0
	CONSTANTA	100.0	66.0	1,800.0	666.0
	ODESSA	50.0	21.7	1,400.0	650.0
	ROSOV-ON-DON	28.0	22.9	50.0	0.0
	NOVOROSSIYSK	200.0	154.0	1,600.0	755.0
	BATUMI	20.0	2.9	200.0	116.1
	POTI	63.0	6.3	550.0	510.0

continued on next page

Table 2 continued

	Port Name	Port Capacity (mtpa)	Combined Throughput (mt)	Container capacity ('000 TEU pa)	Containerized Throughput ('000 TEU)
Caspian Sea	AKTAU	15.0	3.2	25.0	14.3
	KURYK	6.0	2.4	100.0	0.0
	BAKU-ALAT	15.0	4.6	500.0	35.1
	TURKMENBASHI	17.0	8.3	400.0	19.0
	BANDAR AZALI	7.0	1.0	40.0	3.3
	ASTRAKHAN	12.1	2.2	10.0	2.6
Arabian Sea / Indian Ocean	BANDAR ABBAS	130.0	100.0	3,300.0	2,600.0
	CHABAHAR	8.5	3.1	100.0	25.0
	JEBEL ALI	240.0	180.0	19,300.0	14,100.0
	KARACHI	150.00	46.9	4,850.0	2,160.0
	MHD BIN QASIM	90.00	49.0	2,025.0	1,000.0
	GWDAR	5.50	0.1	500.0	4.5
	NHAVA SHEVA	118.90	71.0	7,700.0	5,050.0
	KANDLA	180.00	115.4	600.0	244.0
Pacific Ocean	LIANYUNGANG	330.00	228.0	6,700.0	4,745.0
	TIANJIN	680.00	433.0	20,000.0	15,040.0
	VOSTOCHNY	60.00	28.0	650.0	419.0
	VLADIVOSTOK	12.00	7.5	820.0	680.8
	BUSAN	990.00	400.0	23,000.0	20,660.0

CAREC = Central Asia Regional Economic Cooperation, mt = metric ton, TEU = twenty-foot equivalent unit, pa = per annum.

Source: Findaport.com, World Port Source, Lloyds List Maritime and Port Authorities. Data from latest available year. More detailed information can be found in Volume II.

3. Regional Background

Ports and logistics corridors in CAREC area have been defined by a series of geographic, historic, institutional, and geostrategic factors making it a quite unique part of the world. It is a region that has thrived from trade for centuries, to be almost sealed off the rest of the world in other periods, and again to be at the crossroads of busy trade routes.

3.1. Geography and Historical Legacies

Geography, both physical and human, reach extremes in our area of study. Endless plains in some countries, and some of the highest and less practicable mountain ranges in other. Vast empty areas are found in Mongolia or Kazakhstan and some of the highest population densities along the Indus valley in Pakistan. Despite long distances, the vast plains of Xinjian, Kazakhstan, and the Russian Federation have become busy corridors for east–west trade, while the Karakoram, Tian Shan, Pamir, and associated ranges are still major barriers that limit north–south trade.

A shared history of empires built and dismembered as well as the impact of modern geopolitics has left a legacy of conflicts and human barriers to trade and movement of goods. A non-exhaustive list of closed or almost-closed borders that hamper flows of goods includes Armenia with Azerbaijan, Georgia with the Russian Federation in Abkhazia and Ossetia, or India with Pakistan. Additionally, moving goods to and from or across Iran has been drastically reduced as a result of sanctions, as well as in and out or across Afghanistan as a result of security concerns. One of the more populated areas in Central Asia, the Fergana Valley, is a jigsaw of border lines that imply that basic products that could be sourced a stone throw away need to be delivered through an official border crossing located dozens of kilometers afar.

These are some factors that explain why Central Asia is perceived as one of the areas in the world with higher logistics costs 20% of gross domestic product on average (e.g., 18% in Kazakhstan and 23% in Tajikistan) while they are 9% in countries of the Organization for Economic Co-operation and Development (ITF 2019).

3.2. Increasingly Busy Corridors

Despite the challenges, Central Asia is currently one of the few hot spots in the world where cargo flows grow double digits.[2] Some prospective studies forecast that freight flows in some corridors could increase threefold by 2050, in particular transit flows between the PRC and Europe by rail that grew from less than 7,000 twenty-foot equivalent units (TEU) in 2010, to 150,000 in 2016 and more than 300,000 in 2019. The number of trains on Eurasian rail freight transit grew from 308 trains in 2014 to 4,400 in 2018 (UIC 2020). Still about 98% of volumes on the PRC–EU route move by sea. However, the volume of cargoes that, because of their nature or time sensitivity, could shift from sea transport to rail on the land corridor Asia–Europe has been estimated to amount up to 5.4 million TEU (EDB 2019).

About 70% of the PRC–Europe land freight traffic are moved through Kazakhstan's two rail border crossing points with the PRC, and only 30% through the Trans-Siberian and/or Trans-Mongolian lines. However, the Russian Federation's railways are also busy capturing traffic from Japan and the Republic of Korea to Europe and vice-versa. Current infrastructure plans in CAREC countries are expected to improve connectivity and efficiency but might not be sufficient to accommodate all future growth.

Also, as will be discussed later in Chapter 6 infrastructure planning and practice in most CAREC countries suffer from some weaknesses and are affected by political decisions that may lead to unwise allocation of resources.

---

[2] It is to be noted that this report was conceived and drafted before the COVID-19 pandemic.

3.3. Disappointing Logistics Performance

Most CAREC countries show low scores in the World Bank's Logistics Performance Index (LPI). Eight of the eleven CAREC countries are ranked below the 100th position among the 167 countries assessed by the World Bank, only three are ranked above: the PRC[3] (ranked 27), Kazakhstan (ranked 77), and Pakistan (ranked 95).[4]

Comparing CAREC countries LPI scores with those of their income group it appears that the PRC clearly outperforms the average in its income group. Kazakhstan, the Kyrgyz Republic, Uzbekistan, and Tajikistan score slightly above or close to their respective income groups. The remaining six CAREC countries, Azerbaijan, Georgia, Turkmenistan, Mongolia, Pakistan, and Afghanistan score below their income groups.

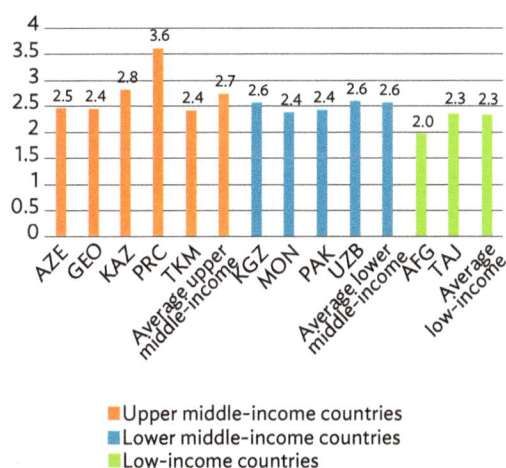

Figure 9: CAREC Countries Logistics Performance Index Benchmarked with their Income Group

- Upper middle-income countries
- Lower middle-income countries
- Low-income countries

AFG = Afghanistan, AZE = Azerbaijan, CAREC = Central Asia Regional Economic Cooperation KAZ = Kazakhstan, KGZ = Kyrgyz Republic, MON = Mongolia, PAK = Pakistan, TAJ = Tajikistan, UZB = Uzbekistan.

Source: World Bank Logistics Performance Index (LPI). The Aggregated LPI is considered, Latest data available on Nov 2020. https://lpi.worldbank.org/

Infrastructure could explain some of these differences but not all. Except for the PRC and Pakistan, scoring clearly above, Tajikistan and Uzbekistan scoring close to the average, the remaining five CAREC countries score below their income group in logistics competences. Also with the exception of the PRC and Pakistan, the remaining nine score below their income group in international shipments.

Border crossing remains a structural concern for seamless trade and transport in CAREC countries. The CAREC corridor performance measuring and monitoring (CPMM) provides good insights on times and costs required at border crossing points. Looking at the CPMM's 8 year-series from 2010 to 2018, the picture that appears is a consistent improvement of speed without delays (SWOD) in all the period, i.e., better infrastructure allows higher speed; but a stagnant to declining trend for speed with delays (SWD), i.e., all time gained before reaching borders is lost once one gets there.

Encouragingly the last 4-year series show improvement in SWD in rail (strong) and in road (weaker). The situation is variable in various corridors as will be further discussed later.

3.4. Railways Playing a Pivotal Role in Logistics Chains

Logistics in most of the study area is characterized by high rail share if compared with other regions in the world. Rail share in terms of Tons per Kilometer (Tn*Km) in Central Asia is 40%, quite above 18% rail share in the EU.[5] This is explained by several factors such as long distances, raw materials as main transported commodities, and the legacy of the former Soviet Union's infrastructure planning that made railways the default transport mode for many flows.

---

[3] It should be noted that only the PRC autonomous regions of Xinjiang–Uighur (XUAR) and Inner Mongolia (IMAR) are properly forming part of CAREC.

[4] It is to be noted that LPI ranks and scores may suffer important yearly oscillations. Also, that not all scores are available for all years in all countries.

[5] Railways modal share in Tn*Km in 2015 was 60% in Kazakhstan, 59% in Mongolia and 40% in Uzbekistan (Sourced from ITF 2019). In the EU, it was 17.9% in 2017 (sourced from Eurostat).

Figure 10: Benchmark of Specific Logistics Performance Index Scores in CAREC Countries

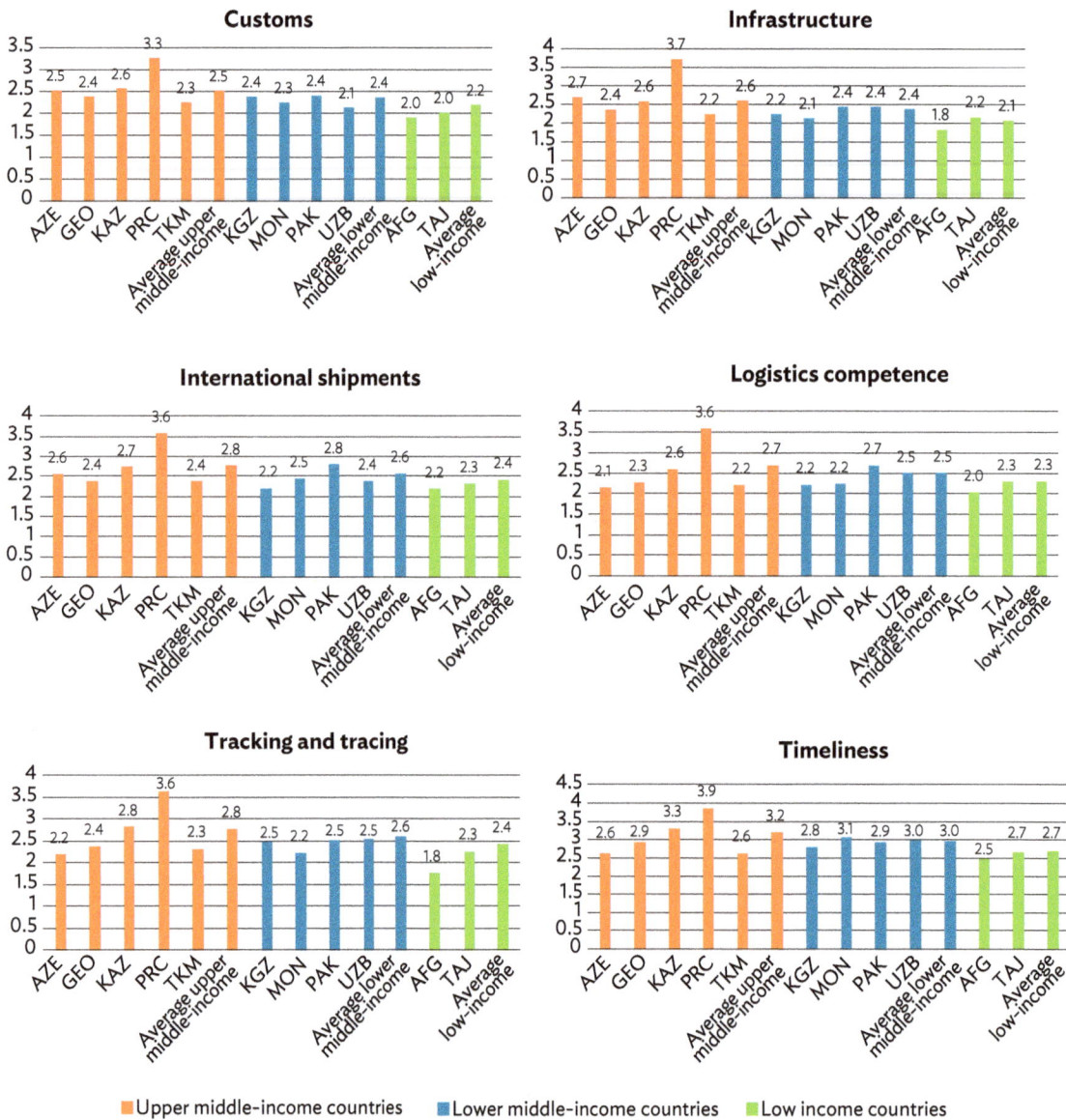

Customs

AZE 2.5, GEO 2.4, KAZ 2.6, PRC 3.3, TKM 2.3, Average upper middle-income 2.5, KGZ 2.4, MON 2.3, PAK 2.4, UZB 2.1, Average lower middle-income 2.4, AFG 2.0, TAJ 2.0, Average low-income 2.2

Infrastructure

AZE 2.7, GEO 2.4, KAZ 2.6, PRC 3.7, TKM 2.2, Average upper middle-income 2.6, KGZ 2.2, MON 2.1, PAK 2.4, UZB 2.4, Average lower middle-income 2.4, AFG 1.8, TAJ 2.2, Average low-income 2.1

International shipments

AZE 2.6, GEO 2.4, KAZ 2.7, PRC 3.6, TKM 2.4, Average upper middle-income 2.8, KGZ 2.2, MON 2.5, PAK 2.8, UZB 2.4, Average lower middle-income 2.6, AFG 2.2, TAJ 2.3, Average low-income 2.4

Logistics competence

AZE 2.1, GEO 2.3, KAZ 2.6, PRC 3.6, TKM 2.2, Average upper middle-income 2.7, KGZ 2.2, MON 2.2, PAK 2.7, UZB 2.5, Average lower middle-income 2.5, AFG 2.0, TAJ 2.3, Average low-income 2.3

Tracking and tracing

AZE 2.2, GEO 2.4, KAZ 2.8, PRC 3.6, TKM 2.3, Average upper middle-income 2.8, KGZ 2.5, MON 2.2, PAK 2.5, UZB 2.5, Average lower middle-income 2.6, AFG 1.8, TAJ 2.3, Average low-income 2.4

Timeliness

AZE 2.6, GEO 2.9, KAZ 3.3, PRC 3.9, TKM 2.6, Average upper middle-income 3.2, KGZ 2.8, MON 3.1, PAK 2.9, UZB 3.0, Average lower middle-income 3.0, AFG 2.5, TAJ 2.7, Average low-income 2.7

■ Upper middle-income countries   ■ Lower middle-income countries   ■ Low income countries

AFG = Afghanistan, AZE = Azerbaijan, CAREC = Central Asia Regional Economic Cooperation, KAZ = Kazakhstan, KGZ = Kyrgyz Republic, MON = Mongolia, PAK = Pakistan, TAJ = Tajikistan, UZB = Uzbekistan.

Source: World Bank Logistics Performance Index. Latest data available on Nov. 2020 https://lpi.worldbank.org/.

However, CAREC countries railways throughput is modest except Kazakhstan's. China Rail throughput is ten times bigger than Kazakhstan's but just a fraction is relevant to CAREC flows. As a matter of comparison, the combined rail throughput of the nine CAREC countries except Kazakhstan, and the PRC is smaller than Germany's (Europe's flagship of rail freight) but bigger than that of Iran or Turkey.

The opening of several pipelines in recent years has reduced volumes of crude oil and hydrocarbons transported by rail. Traffic in CAREC and in the PRC is recovering slowly after declines in 2011–2014 and still performing better that Germany, EU flagship for rail freight. The Russian Federation and Iran railways show a much clearer upward trend.

Figure 11: Speed to Travel on CAREC Corridors

Eight-Year Series

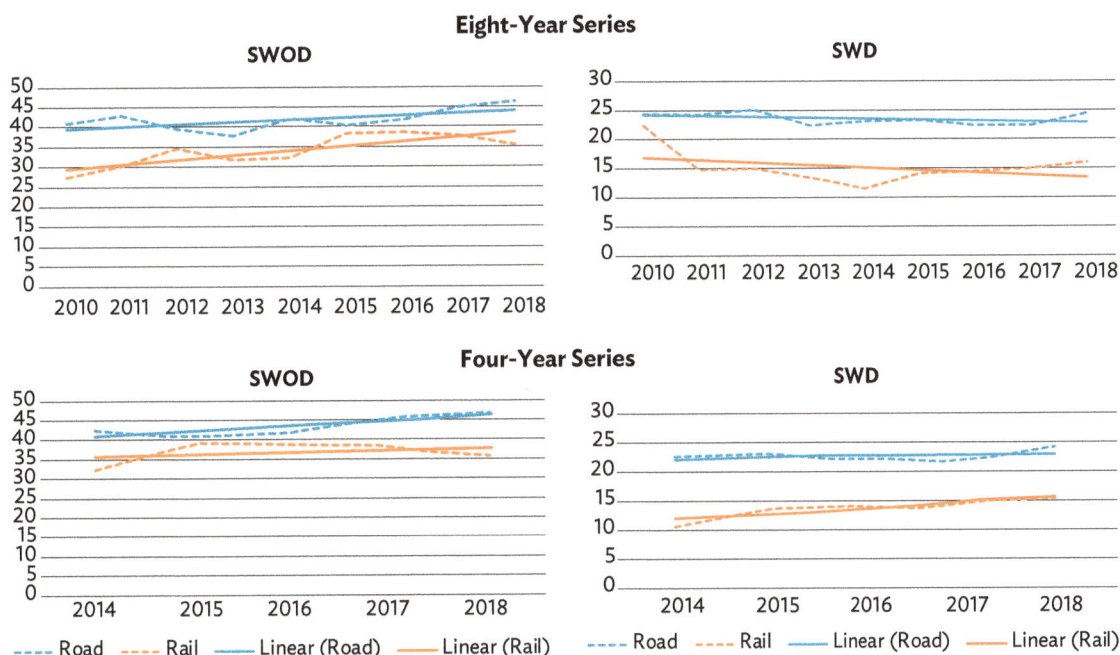

CAREC = Central Asia Regional Economic Cooperation, SWD = speed with delay, SWOD = speed without delay.

Source: CAREC Corridor Performance Measuring and Monitoring 2018.

Figure 12: Benchmark of CAREC Countries' Freight Rail Throughput

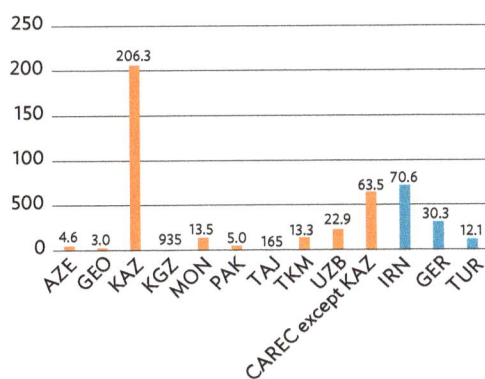

AZE = Azerbaijan, CAREC = Central Asia Regional Economic Cooperation, GEO = Georgia, KAZ = Kazakhstan, KGZ = Kyrgyz Republic, MON = Mongolia, PAK = Pakistan, TAJ = Tajikistan, TKM = Turkmenistan, UZB = Uzbekistan.

Million ton*km. Data from 2017.

Source: World Bank database. https://lpi.worldbank.org/

Rail throughput in terms of Tn*Km for 2010–2017 grew in Kazakhstan, Mongolia, and Pakistan; kept more or less stable in Uzbekistan, the Kyrgyz Republic, and Turkmenistan; and experienced substantial decline in Azerbaijan, Georgia, and Tajikistan.[6]

However, the reality in Commonwealth Independent State (CIS) countries is that not all countries are naturally at the same position to benefit or promote at the same level from railways inherited from the former Soviet Union. Typically, the Kyrgyz Republic and Tajikistan railways are captive to Kazakhstan and Uzbekistan and act as end-lines to these bigger networks. While in Tajikistan, the primary line is for Talco Plant connecting to Uzbekistan, the network in the Kyrgyz Republic consists of short distance split lines connected to Kazakhstan. Unless new lines with the PRC are constructed, they would continue to be dependent on countries with bigger networks. However, due to mountainous terrain and small national markets, the financial feasibility of these new lines is dubious.

[6] Source: Presentation by Tyrrell Duncan, Technical Assistance team leader: Report on Railway Sector Assessments at CAREC Railway Working Group in Bangkok, December 2019. In the case of Azerbaijan, capital repairs were made to augment capacity according to government sources.

Figure 13: Rail Traffic Trends CAREC and Other Benchmark Countries
(in million tons per kilometer)

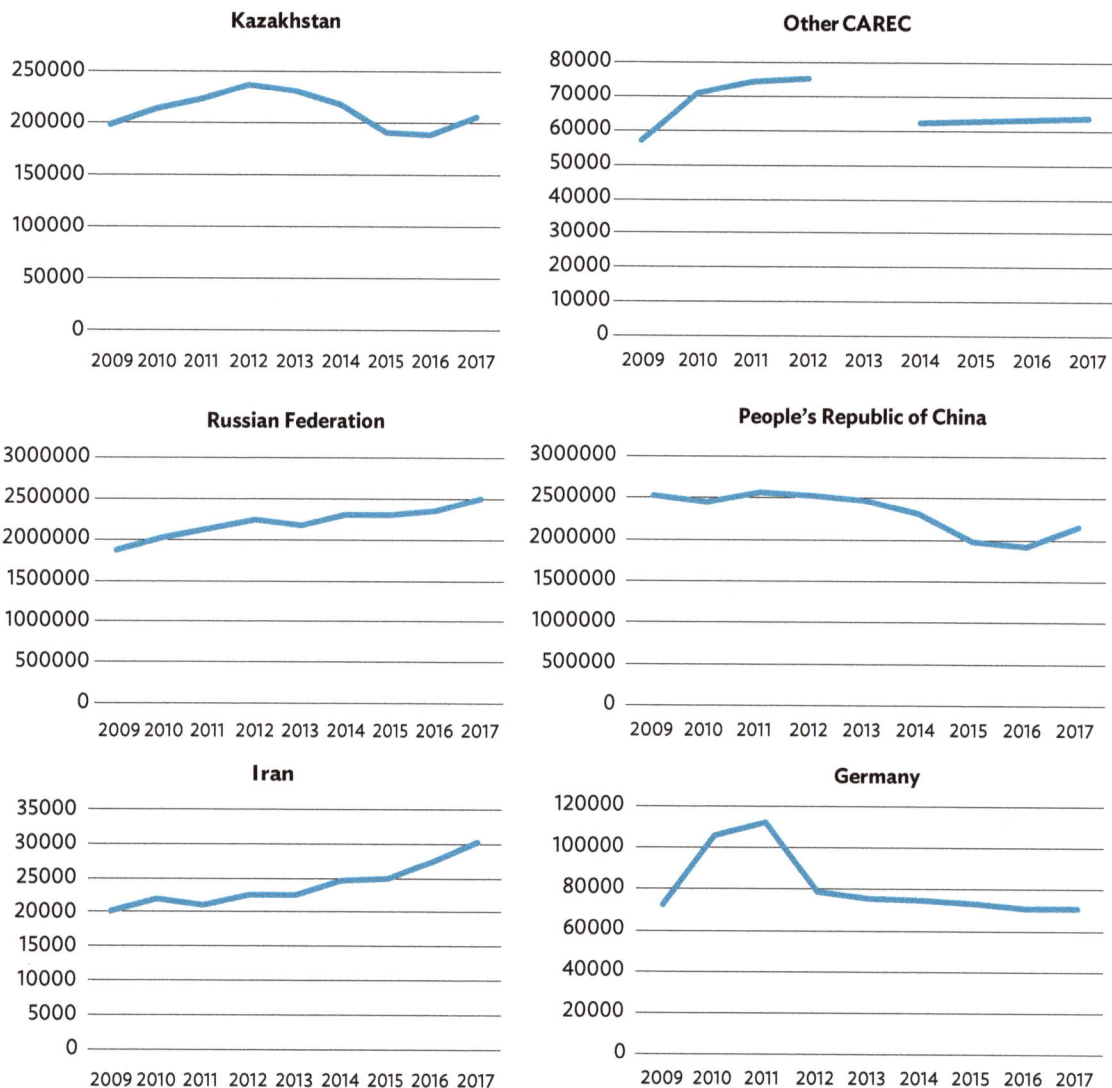

Kazakhstan

Other CAREC

Russian Federation

People's Republic of China

Iran

Germany

CAREC = Central Asia Regional Economic Cooperation.

Source: World Bank database.

Rail in most CAREC countries is still dominated by bulk cargo of minerals, grains, oil, and derivates, etc. Accordingly, there are few and sometimes inappropriate facilities to handle intermodal, i.e., combined transport rail–road of containers, swap bodies, etc. Container traffic developing in flows with PRC but still marginal across the trans-Caucasus/trans-Caspian routes as well as in the north–south corridors across Pakistan or Iran.

Some CAREC countries have implemented reforms in their railway sectors being transformed from government agencies into public sector corporations with, in theory, looser political interference, and higher commercial autonomy. Despite these changes, most railways are still struggling to overcome entrenched legacy inertias and develop an open, transparent, and commercial corporate culture. Most railways suffer from productivity issues, sometimes obsolete and not optimal use of rolling stock, overstaffing, and reliance on transport of bulk and semibulk commodities.

Rail freight tariffs in some countries are being subsidized to attract customers and develop corridors though the amount of subsidy is obscured in non-transparent accounts.[7] It is worth to wonder about the long-term sustainability of these schemes, the impact on volumes once they disappear, and the burden on the finances of the involved railways and other stakeholders. More so since quite often, revenue from freight business, usually loosely regulated by governments, cross-subsidizes passenger services with government-imposed low fares and loss-making public service obligations. On the opposite side, railways tariffs in other corridors, presumably with captive markets, appear to be quite high, even higher than road.[8]

A further challenge for east–west railway traffic is different rules and standards. The Organization for the Cooperation among Railways (OSJD)[9] sets standards for railways communications, standards and consignment notes (SMGS) in all CAREC countries, except Pakistan, plus the Russian Federation and the PRC. However, most countries in Western Europe plus, Turkey, Iran, and Afghanistan use the Convention Concerning International Carriage by Rail (COTIF) standards and Contract of International Carriage of Goods by Rail (CIM) consignment note. Most European countries that were members of the former Soviet Union use both standards. A joint CIM/SMGS consignment note has been developed in paper and electronic format to allow seamless movement using a single consignment note. A Unified Rail Law is also being developed to promote Euro-Asian rail flows.

Many countries across the world are setting up strategies to promote higher use of rail freight transport as part of their climate change commitments and aiming at reducing their dependency on fossil fuels (more so where they are imported). Having a high rail share is already an advantage for CAREC countries while most other regions in the world are struggling to maintain, not to mention, increase rail share.

3.5   International Cooperation Frameworks and Geopolitics

Ports and logistics in CAREC countries cannot be fully understood without looking at the complex web of regional cooperation frameworks involving trade and transport facilitation agreements and mechanisms that influence how goods move to and from ports to Eurasia hinterlands.

3.5.1. Commonwealth of Independent States

Most CAREC countries were once part of the former Soviet Union and later members of the looser CIS structure. Under the umbrella of CIS, members of the former Soviet Union agreed basic regulatory standards to ensure that the seamless movement of trains and trucks that was possible in the past was maintained for the newly independent republics.

Key regulatory standards relevant for our study are set by OSJD (see previous section) and the Minsk Agreement in 1999 on the masses and dimensions of vehicles. However, harmonization in truck dimensions is not complete since some countries have set exemptions to some of its clauses or additional requirements. Though Minsk standards are not far away from those applied in Turkey and most of Europe differences exist and some countries, e.g. Georgia, are moving to full harmonization with EU standards. Indeed some stakeholders mention the Minsk Agreement as a barrier to wider Eurasian harmonization.

3.5.2. Transport Corridor Europe Caucasus Asia

This EU-sponsored initiative was launched in 1993 with the strategic objective of bringing members of the former Soviet Union closer to Europe by developing infrastructure and trade routes on land and across the Black and Caspian seas. The Transport Corridor Europe Caucasus Asia (TRACECA) was stablished as an Intergovernmental commission with a permanent Secretariat in Baku. Its members are Armenia, Azerbaijan, Bulgaria, Georgia, Iran,

---

[7] This is particularly happening in the PRC to promote PRC–Europe rail freight. Subsidies are also offered to attract traffic to the Middle Corridor across the Caspian and Caucasus.

[8] CPMM 2018 shows that this seems to be happening on CAREC Corridors 4 and 6 and in some countries e.g., Mongolia, Turkmenistan, and Uzbekistan.

[9] OSJD. http://en.osjd.org.

Kazakhstan, the Kyrgyz Republic, Moldova, Romania, Tajikistan, Turkey, Ukraine and Uzbekistan.[10]

TRACECA has developed about 84 projects in infrastructure, rolling stock, and trade facilitation that received €215 million of EU assistance up to 2016. In 2009 a Multimodal Transport Agreement was signed setting a unified legal framework for the development of multimodal transport. Since 2016, the TRACECA multilateral permits for road transport have been applied among six TRACECA countries. Also, a Regional Action Strategy on Maritime Safety and Security and Environmental Protection up to 2021 is being implemented. More initiatives on streamlining the border crossing procedures and cargo traffic are being promoted.

TRACECA pioneered the concept of transnational cooperation for corridor development in this region and some of its key objectives have been achieved such as:

(i)   Construction of direct rail link between Central Asia and Turkey trough Baku–Tbilisi–Kars (BTK) railway.
(ii)   Upgrading of most major Caspian ports in Azerbaijan, Kazakhstan, and Turkmenistan, permitting much more efficient cargo flows.
(iii)   Lay the seed for more operational corridor promotion organizations such as TITR/TMTM that is actively promoting cargoes on the corridor Kazakhstan–Black Sea/Turkey ("Middle Corridor").[11]

3.5.3. Eurasian Economic Union

The Economic Union members are the Russian Federation, Belarus, Armenia, Kazakhstan, and the Kyrgyz Republic.[12] The Eurasian Economic Union (EAEU) has eliminated customs clearance between members of the Union.[13]

However, the drawback is that a shipment from Nakhodka or St. Petersburg to Almaty or Bishkek will move through a single customs territory, and if it goes to Tashkent it will go through two customs territories. However, the same shipment coming from Poti to Almaty or Bishkek will cross three customs territories and if it is bound to Tashkent it will be crossing four customs territories.

Similarly, shipments from Khorgos to the EU though Kazakhstan, the Russian Federation, and Belarus will move across only two customs territories (EAEU and EU), while if using the "Middle Corridor" it will move across four (EAEU, AZE, GEO, and EU).

3.5.4. The Belt and Road Initiative

The Belt and Road Initiative (BRI) is a PRC-sponsored initiative that has defined six main economic corridors, four of them within the geographic scope of this study. They are:

1: Eurasia Land Bridge Economic Corridor
2: PRC, Mongolia, Russian Federation Economic Corridor
3: PRC, Central Asia, West Asia Economic Corridor
4. PRC, Pakistan Economic Corridor.

Corridors 5 and 6 are beyond the scope of this study.

There is no entity nor official list compiling BRI transport projects, not any criteria to assess what is BRI and what is not. However, a recent World Bank study (WB 2019) estimated investment in transport infrastructure up to $144 billion in 70 countries. Most of it corresponds to projects within the area of this scoping study though the precise share is hard to determine.

World Bank estimates reductions in travel times by up to 12% and increase trade by 5.2% as a result of implementing all these projects. Average shipment times between the PRC and Central Asia are expected to be reduced from 15 to 13 days once all BRI projects are implemented and that benefits of transport infrastructure are likely to be felt mostly in Kazakhstan, the Kyrgyz Republic, Tajikistan, and Pakistan.

---

[10] Turkmenistan was a beneficiary of the European Union's TRACECA program but has never been a member of the Basic Multilateral Agreement—the legal basis of TRACECA.

[11] See: TRACECA. http://www.traceca-org.org/en.

[12] See: Eurasian Economic Union. http://www.eaeunion.org.

[13] Consulted stakeholders on the field missions voiced concerns about hurdles still occurring at some BCPs and some petty corruption. At the time of writing this report, the situation was particularly difficult at BCP between Kazakhstan and the Kyrgyz Republic because of concerns about smuggling of consumer goods from the PRC.

The World Bank and other organizations (OECD 2018); (Marlene Laruelle, 2018); (EBRD 2019); (Peace-Nexus 2019) have alerted about the need to carefully assess projects and the impacts on a country's indebtedness. Moreover, it is highlighted that infrastructure projects need to be accompanied by soft reforms and trade facilitation to reap full benefits. Another concern is that BRI projects may emphasize Central Asia as a transit territory between the PRC and Europe rather than focus on connecting Central Asia to world markets.

3.5.5. The European Union Partnership

Among CAREC countries, Azerbaijan and Georgia are members of the European Union Eastern Partnership together with Armenia, Moldova, Belarus, and Ukraine. Turkey stands a step ahead, being officially recognized the status of "accession country." This involves progressive alignment with EU regulations in several fields such as transport and customs in view of strengthening links with the EU bloc and pave the way to an eventual accession. This is slowly moving regulations in these countries closer to the EU legislative acquis and potentially drifting them away from the CIS framework.

As an example, both Azerbaijan and Georgia are in the process of certifying compliance to adopt the New Computerized Transit System (NCTS), the transit procedure used for customs transit operations between the EU member states.

3.5.6. The Economic Cooperation Organization

The Economic Cooperation Organization (ECO) brings together Afghanistan, Azerbaijan, Iran, Kazakhstan, the Kyrgyz Republic, Pakistan, Tajikistan, Turkey, Turkmenistan, and Uzbekistan and is headquartered in Tehran.

Transport and connectivity are among top priorities of ECO to materialize enhanced cooperation for economic growth and development through maximizing connectivity, mobility, and accessibility and making major ECO transport corridors commercially viable and operational. ECO is engaged in the implementation of a Transit Transport Framework Agreement (TTFA), which entered into force in 2006.

The organization is active in promoting the development of transport corridors such as container train routes Islamabad–Tehran–Istanbul, Bandar Abbas–Almaty and other corridors such as Iran–Turkmenistan–Kazakhstan and Iran–Azerbaijan–Russian Federation.

3.5.7. The Shanghai Cooperation Organization

The program of multilateral trade and economic cooperation of the Shanghai Cooperation Organization (SCO) member countries regulates the development of cooperation in the transport sector. To this end some interaction mechanism has been created—the Meeting of Ministers of Transport and the Ad Hoc Working Group on the Transit Potential Development (AWG).

In 2014, in the framework of the SCO, an intergovernmental agreement "On creating favourable conditions for international road transport" was signed. The Asian Development Bank (ADB) and the United Nations Economic and Social Commission for Asia and the Pacific took an active part in the preparation of the document. The main objectives of the agreement are to create favorable conditions for road transport; coordination of countries' efforts for their development and simplification and harmonization of documentation, procedures and requirements in transportation. The agreement regulates the start of implementation, no later than the period 2018–2020 of international road transport along six routes through certain border crossing points at state borders, most coinciding with CAREC's corridor map.

Among the CAREC countries, SCO members are the PRC, Kazakhstan, Tajikistan, the Kyrgyz Republic, Uzbekistan, and Pakistan; SCO observer state status granted to Afghanistan and Mongolia; being Azerbaijan a dialogue partner.

3.5.8. United Nations Economic Commission for Europe and United Nations Economic and Social Commission for Asia and the Pacific

United Nations Economic Commission for Europe

Under the framework of the United Nations Economic Commission for Europe (UNECE), a number of agreements have been achieved that have modeled standards for inland transport not only in Europe but in the former Soviet Union, Central and South Asia, Middle East, and North Africa and beyond. Some of these are highlighted:

(i)   European Agreements on Main International Traffic Arteries (AGR), Main International Railway Lines (AGC) and International Combined Transport Lines and related Installations (AGTC).

(ii) Transport operations-related conventions for dangerous goods by road (ADR), perishable foodstuffs (ATP), Contract of international carriage by road (CMR) and concerning the work of crews of vehicles engaged in international road transport (AETR).

(iii) Border Crossing Facilitation conventions, in particular TIR Convention and the Convention on the Harmonization of Frontier Controls of Goods (HFCG). Euro-Asian Transport Links (EATL) is a joint undertaking between UNECE and UNESCAP set up in 2002 and has identified key priority Euro-Asian road and rail routes. A GIS application of these corridors is available and an International Transport Infrastructure Observatory for EATL corridors was expected to be completed by the end of 2020.

As can be seen in Figure 14, few CAREC countries have joined AGC, AGR and AGTC. Also, harmonization of rules regarding road transportation of hazardous freight under ADR and foodstuff (ATP)

Figure 14: CAREC Countries as Contracting Parties of UNECE Conventions

	AGC	AGR	AGTC	ADR	ATP	CMR	AETR	TIR	HFCG	EATL
AFG	Red	Red	Red	Red	Red	Red	Red	Green	Red	Green
AZE	Green	Green	Red	Green	Green	Green	Green	Green	Green	Green
GEO	Green	Green	Green	Green	Green	Green	Green	Green	Green	Green
KAZ	Green	Green	Green	Green	Green	Green	Green	Green	Green	Green
KGZ	Red	Red	Red	Red	Red	Green	Red	Green	Green	Green
MON	Red	Red	Red	Red	Red	Green	Green	Green	Green	Green
PAK	Red	Red	Red	Red	Red	Green	Green	Green	Red	Green
PRC	Red	Red	Red	Red	Red	Red	Green	Green	Red	Green
TAJ	Red	Red	Red	Red	Red	Green	Green	Green	Green	Green
TKM	Green	Green	Red	Red	Red	Red	Green	Green	Green	Green
UZB	Red	Red	Red	Green	Green	Green	Green	Green	Green	Green

ADR = Agreement concerning the International Carriage of Dangerous Goods by Road, AETR = European Agreement Concerning the Work of Crews of Vehicles Engaged in International Road Transport, AFG = Afghanistan, AGC = European Agreement on Main International Railway Lines, AGTC = European Agreement on Important International Combined Transport Lines and Related Installations, AZE = Azerbaijan, CAREC = Central Asia Regional Economic Cooperation, CMR = Contract for the International Carriage of Goods by Road, EATL = Euro-Asian Transport Links, GEO = Georgia, HFCG = Convention on the Harmonization of Frontier Controls of Goods, KAZ = Kazakhstan, KGZ = Kyrgyz Republic, MON = Mongolia, PAK = Pakistan, PRC = People's Republic of China, TAJ = Tajikistan, TIR = Customs Convention on the International Transport of Goods under Cover, TKM = Turkmenistan, UZB = Uzbekistan.

Contracting parties are shown in green. If not - in red.

Source: UNECE. https://unece.org/transport.

is not complete. However, all CAREC countries are TIR contracting parties though Pakistan and the PRC acceded the TIR convention only in 2018 and implementation is in progress.

United Nations Economic and Social Commission for Asia and the Pacific

In 2016, UNESCAP's Transport Committee adopted the Regional Action Program for Sustainable Transport Connectivity in the Asia-Pacific Region (Phase I is designed for 2017–2021). ESCAP is working on the further development and expansion of intergovernmental agreements "On the Asian Highway Network" (AHN), "On the Trans-Asian Railway Network" (TARN) and "On Dry Ports" (DP).

3.5.9. Other Agreements

Some CAREC countries are also members of a variety of other regional agreements, plus multiple bilateral transport and trade agreements. The most relevant of those regional and multinational agreements are:

(i)   The South Asian Association for Regional Cooperation: Afghanistan, Bangladesh, Bhutan, India, the Maldives, Nepal, Pakistan, and Sri Lanka.
(ii) The Ashgabat Agreement: India, Iran, Kazakhstan, Oman, Uzbekistan, and Turkmenistan
(iii) The Quadrilateral Transport and Trade Agreement: The PRC, the Kyrgyz Republic, Kazakhstan, and Pakistan.
(iv) The Turkic Council: Azerbaijan, Kazakhstan, the Kyrgyz Republic, Turkey, and Uzbekistan.

Figure 15: CAREC Countries as Contracting Parties of UNESCAP Agreements

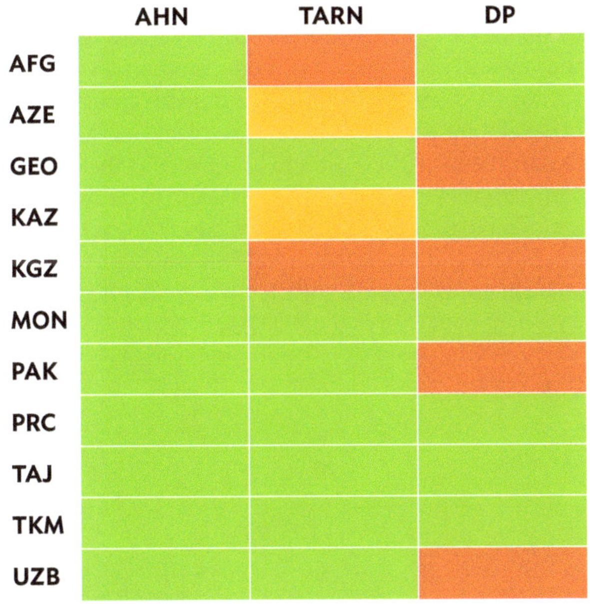

AHN = Asian Highway Network, AFG = Afghanistan, AZE = Azerbaijan, CAREC = Central Asia Regional Economic Cooperation, DP = Dry Ports, GEO = Georgia, KAZ = Kazakhstan, KGZ = Kyrgyz Republic, MON = Mongolia, PAK = Pakistan, PRC = People's Republic of China, TAJ = Tajikistan, TKM = Turkmenistan, UZB = Uzbekistan.

Contracting parties are shown in green. If not - in red. In orange - signatories of the agreement but pending approval, acceptance or ratification.

Source: UNESCAP. https://www.unescap.org/.

4. Identified Issues at CAREC Ports

Volume II of this report includes a description of the most relevant ports, both at CAREC and non-CAREC countries, at the head or serving the abovementioned corridors, including ports at the Caspian Sea. Main technical characteristics, capacity, volumes, governance, landside connectivity, key announced investments, and main shipping routes are described. Particular attention is paid to the role these ports are currently playing as gateways for CAREC countries and their future potential and ambitions.

This section includes some high-level observation and analysis of ports and shipping exclusively in CAREC countries. It is to be noted that since Caspian ports and shipping are intrinsically embedded into multimodal land corridors, they will also be treated in Chapter 5.

4.1. Institutional and Governance Issues at Ports

High-level institutional frameworks for the governance of ports and maritime sectors in most CAREC coastal countries show different types of problems. In some cases, the institutional governance framework is weak and fragmented (e.g., Georgia), in others, it is dominated by operational players such as railways (e.g., Kazakhstan). In other ports, governance and reform are hampered by a myriad of vested interests (e.g., Pakistan). Fragmented concessions and control over port services can lead to duplication of effort and displaced institutional and governance issues.

At ports level there is evidence that old systems of governance have been retained that are not fully capable of meeting the modern needs of port development and management. Though nominally most ports in CAREC countries appear to follow the standard Landlord Port management model, there are evidences of shortcomings in ensuring appropriate competition for the market and competition in the market, as well as equal opportunities for all players.

Ports in most developed countries are evolving from the administrative mindset that usually characterizes the landlord paradigm into a more commercial approach, positioning themselves as leading partners in developing a port-related industrial and logistics cluster (Langen 2020). It is to acknowledge that some top management in CAREC ports seem to be aware of the need to progress into this new paradigm, but lack a supporting institutional framework, staff with the appropriate skills, and a sufficiently developed market.

Some examples of this issue are mentioned in Boxes 1–3.

Box 1: Ports and Railways in Kazakhstan

In Kazakhstan, the port services have been regarded as a servant to the railways. This is demonstrated in the management procedures for ports where the rail networks are directly connected to the port and shipping must wait for railway arrivals to complete loading timetables. The railways company KTZ JSC has a 100% stake in the Kuryk port company and has various stakes at both Port of Aktau and North Terminal. Moreover, KTZ JSC is the largest transport and logistics operator in Kazakhstan and has direct or indirect stakes in logistics and transportation companies, owners of terminals and main infrastructure of all modes of transport.

New port. The Kuryk new port railways ferry terminal is now being used in Kazakhstan (photo by consultants).

Source: Consultants Field Trip.

Box 2: Ports Governance in Georgia

In Georgia, there is a combination of situations: (i) a freehold arrangement in Poti port, where APM Terminals is the beneficial owner and major operator (with PACE as secondary operator); (ii) Batumi port, where land is government-owned but management rights awarded to Kazakhstan's SOE KazTransOil, that itself leases terminal operations to third parties; (iii) Kulevi oil terminal is owned and operated by Azerbaijan's Oil Company (SOCAR); and (iv) Supsa terminal is operated by BP but final beneficiary is the government.

The result of lessening Georgian state interests and a variety of ad-hoc arrangements in the maritime sector is that there is a void in government regulation of ports and maritime activity. In some sense Georgia is trying to correct this imbalance with the establishment of the Maritime Training Academy in 2011 with a mandate to create a sustainable maritime system in Georgia. However, its immediate tasks are to build industry capacity to issue certificates of competency for seafarers and help the Georgian shipping fleet obtain technical certificates for international operations. Nevertheless, the absence of a national regulatory focus and legislative mandates for port operations and compliance remains a growing problem in Georgia.

Source: Consultants Field Trip.

Box 3: Karachi Ports Reform

In Pakistan, the regulatory controls in the ports and maritime area are wide in their theoretical scope. Pakistani ports are administered by trusts and authorities which report to the Ministry of Ports and Shipping. Pakistan port administrators have long struggled to move ahead a reform agenda, particularly at Karachi Ports Trust (KPT). However, legacy issues seem to be hampering a full transition to a landlord model, allowing private sector contracts for harbor towage, dredging of channels, pilotage, and stevedoring of bulk cargoes. Instead, KPT maintains full services for nearly all port functions, purchases capital equipment, and employs full time staff and management. It could also be said that, port development and planning at KPT is restricted given the segregation from direct involvement in hinterland transport access to the port areas. KPT also manages a large portfolio of commercial real estate that reportedly contributes a major part of its operations. An absence of coordination between Pakistan government authorities (Pakistan Railways, National Highways Authority, and Ministry of Ports and Shipping) is evident in developing meaningful improvements to port access for rail and road links. Finally, the strong labor unions in Karachi have been able to resist modernization of work practices and rationalization of workers employed for port labor.

Source: Consultants Field Trip.

4.2.   Aging Infrastructure from Legacy Design Features and Operational Activities

In several CAREC countries the original design features are retained at ports such as Aktau, Batumi, Poti and the river port section of Karachi port. Some of the physical port infrastructure design features in Central Asian countries are similar in characteristic being a legacy of the former Soviet Union era's standardized specifications for ports. These original design features often limit modern operational efficiency due to shortage of laydown areas for containerized freight, narrow wharf areas that limit the manoeuvering of modern mobile plant equipment and wharf pavement that often has limited weight-bearing capacity.

In Aktau port, Batumi and Poti the older operational wharves have rail tracks along their perimeters that are a legacy of the original design features for rail mounted ship-to-shore portal cranes. The modern design features for general cargo and multipurpose cargo wharves is for rubber tyre gantry cranes that offer superior flexibility and can be removed from the wharf frontage to create free space for cargo handling and storage, where and as

Batumi Port. Rail tracks for portal gantry cranes and rail tracks for rail wagons in close proximity to wharf and cargo working areas.

required. The port of Karachi suffers from aging wharf infrastructure and retained warehousing along the perimeter of the bulk and breakbulk wharves. These old facilities coupled with outdated cargo handling processes restrict efficiency and productivity.

There are also some cargo handling procedures retained from past practices that result in low productivity, particularly in handling of loose (uncontainerized) cargoes. Some of the issues are linked to labor laws and labor union legacy agreements.

4.3.   Unresolved Port–City Issues and Land Accessibility

The proximity of ports to their host cities and towns was a positive attribute in the past era. However, in the modern era, the demand for land escalated with the urban growth, which in turn increased the value of waterfront land. This meant that the proximity of port owned waterfront land became highly valued to commercial developers.

Several CAREC countries have reacted to the need to relocate commercial ports away from their original host cities to areas which have uncontested industrial land (e.g., Alat in Azerbaijan or Qasim in Pakistan).

Some examples of these port-city issues are exemplified in Boxes 4–6.

4.4.   Impacts of Caps on Vessel Capacity

Shipping services on the Caspian and Black seas are subject to some physical limitations.

In the Black Sea the shipping needs are met by regular ferry services that provide point-to-point operations and by vessels of between 3,000 TEU and 8,000–9,000 TEU capacity. The smaller ships act as short sea feeders transiting between partner ports located in the same sea region. Restrictions imposed across the Bosphorus Strait limit ship sizes up to 8,000–9,000 TEU for transit from Mediterranean ports into the Black Sea.[14] This is likely to reflect on freight capacity, provision of port handling equipment, and freight rates charged.

---

[14] Under the Montreux Convention of 1936, commercial shipping has the right of free passage through the Straits in peacetime, although Turkey claims the right to impose regulations for safety and environmental purposes.

Box 4: Port Relocation in Azerbaijan

Baku in Azerbaijan is one example where the host city growth began to restrict the freight corridors to the city-side port as well as escalating land values created a dilemma in retaining port activities on high cost real estate. By relocating the commercial shipping activities of Baku to the new port of Alat some 65 kilometers south of the central core of Azerbaijan's capital city, the new port has been designed as a full-fledged intermodal transportation hub including a free trade zone without urban encroachment. The new port at Alat is however underutilized at present with its capacity established in excess of 10 million tonnes per annum and throughout in 2019 only reaching 4.55 million tonnes.

Alat Port. The new port has been designed as full-fledged intermodal transportation hub including a free trade zone without urban encroachment.

Source: Consultants Field Trip.

Box 5: Coexistence of Port and Urban Functions in Batumi

Batumi is a case where urban encroachment reaches right up to the port gate. Container trucks line up on public roads close to the downtown waiting to access the port. Mitigation measures were being planned by port management to alleviate trucks parking on public roads with the expansion of new port access roadways. This may have the downside of reducing public road widths and could still adversely impact traffic in peak times of port activity. In a recent ADB report, Batumi was listed as a multifunctional city with a tourism industry dominant above other economic sectors. This reinforces the need to address urban encroachment on port activities given

Use of public roads. Trucks using public roads as waiting areas at Batumi Port gates.

the value and demand for waterfront land to the future economic development of Batumi, (ADB 2016). Further evidence of urban encroachment on port facilities at Batumi is stated in the 2017 Urban Mobility Plan, which states that the projected port turnover of 47,000–50,000 containers per year may be limited because of the restricted street capacity of Batumi (A+S Consult GmbH 2017).

Source: Consultants Field Trip.

The Black Sea ship size limits may be eventually be overcome with building the proposed Kanal İstanbul, approved by the Turkish environment ministry in 2019. It would be a 45km shipping canal joining the Black Sea to the Marmara, running parallel to the Bosphorus strait. If commissioned, this new canal would allow ships of up to 18,000 TEU capacity to enter the Black Sea, overcoming the need for smaller ships or transhipment operations at Istanbul and Marmara Sea ports. Theoretically this development would then reduce freight costs for ships connecting Black Sea ports with those in the Mediterranean and beyond.

Box 6: Port Access Challenges in Karachi

In Pakistan, the hinterland access to the port of Karachi is severely limited due to urban development and the lack of road and railway capacity to keep pace with the increase in containerized volumes. Long lines of trucks can be found on urban roads leading to the terminals even if Karachi Municipal Corporation has set traffic restrictions for trucks that are often disrespected. The Karachi Port Improvement Project (KPIP) did address the matter of urban encroachment and congestion at Karachi and highlighted improvements required, the recommendations in this report however appear not to have either been endorsed or acted upon, (Maritime & Transport Business Solutions B.V. 2015). Rail corridors linking the port of Karachi have been neglected

Port access challenges. Container trucks at Karachi road leading to terminals.

resulting in urban settlements enveloping tracks and hundreds of uncontrolled railroad crossings.

Currently, Qasim port and only one in three container terminals in Karachi Port have direct operational railway access.

To overcome difficulties and restrictions across the city for port-bound trucks, Pakistan rail (PR) has voiced concept plans to link all three KPT terminals and Qasim ones to a marshalling yard at Pipri where 2,000 acres (around 800 hectares) of land is available for rail and for logistics and industrial development. An off-dock terminal would be built there allowing most container traffic to cross the city by rail instead of trucks. There may be issues with the rail corridor plan as many of the rail freight corridors are either partially or fully encroached by formal or informal dwellings and there are many public road crossings to consider (Shah, 2020). Moreover, various port and private sector stakeholders are doubtful about the benefits of this project.

Source: Consultants Field Trip.

Typical short sea container ship in the Black Sea trading at Poti Port.

Similarly, the Caspian Sea has ship size limitations imposed by the port capacity and depths at berths and/or the capacity of the Volga Don canal, which allows ships to transit to the Black Sea and beyond. Commercial ports operating on the Caspian Sea have an operational draft limit in channels and alongside berths no greater than 6-7 meters (m) (see Caspian ports section on Volume II).

Moreover, a maximum length of 139.95m and a beam of 16.7m is required for Volga-Don Max class of vessels (Marine Engineering Bureau 2020). The draft for inland waterway operations is 3.6m, equating to a deadweight of 4,520 tonnes. For open sea (saline oceans) operations these figures can be increased to a draft of 4.7m and a deadweight of 7,150 tonnes. The Volga-Don cap on size is relevant for various reasons: (i) allows access into the Caspian of vessels built elsewhere; (ii) the canal is the default route for out of gauge cargoes, typically used for the oil and gas industry and other engineering projects; and (iii) bigger vessels could not be deployed in the Black Sea and beyond, thus restricting Caspian shipping companies from providing commercial services to third parties, which seems to be a common practice.[15]

Draft and channel limits residing at Caspian Sea ports would theoretically impose a maximum limit of ship to 13,000 Dead Weight Tonnes (DWT), but even these concept limits could be fully loaded to allow for depth limits alongside berths, (Ghasemi, 2018). The maximum sized Ro/Ro ferries operated by ASCO and Karmortransflot in the Caspian Sea are no larger than 7,000 DWT, except for oil tankers (ASCO 2020).

Consequently, demand must be distributed over a larger fleet of ships rather than operating fleets of fewer but bigger vessels. Therefore, the cost of operation for smaller ferries and smaller commercial ships is higher.

As a matter of comparison, the journey Alat–Aktau takes about 18 hours and costs $1,200 for a truck Ro/Ro operation using vessels with maximum capacity of around 7,000 tons. A similar Ro/Ro journey Barcelona–Genoa would take 7 hours and cost slightly more than $1,000, using a much bigger vessel with a capacity of 30,000–50,000 tons. Thus, from the shipping company standpoint, the yield per transported truck is likely to be lower in the Caspian case.

From the shipper standpoint costs are higher, e.g. shipping a 40-foot equivalent unit (FEU) from Baku to Turkmenbashi (one-way) would cost $1,000 amounting to $6 per nautical mile, while a shipment from Mersin in Southern Turkey to Italy's Trieste costs $1 per nautical mile.

It should be noted that fuel costs and purchasing power are lower at Caspian countries and that the average value of commodities transported is likely to be lower.

Since most trans-Caspian ferry fleet is Government owned it is uncertain up to what extent costs are fully translated to freight charges borne by customers or are borne by governments through subsidies to national shipping companies. In the first case higher transport costs are likely depressing demand. In the second case neither government companies nor the private sector have an incentive to add more ferry services, thus not fully providing an attractive and competitive supply of transport services to shippers.

It is rather possible that both effects, i.e., high freight charges and subsidized losses incurred by shipping companies are happening at the same time on trans-Caspian Sea transport. However, a detailed study on this issue would be recommended.

Similarly, it is uncertain to what extent port fees cover port operations costs or are subsidized. Port fees in Alat, Aktau and Kuryk are about $3,000 per vessel while 15,500 (Ro/Ro) and 6,500–7,200 (rail ferry) in Turkmenbashi.[16] Parity-based discounts have been discussed but not fully implemented.

In any case, capacity caps, in particular, across the Caspian involve an intrinsic restriction to develop efficient, competitive and profitable operations.

In addition, vessels size has another impact. Being smaller, vessels operating in the Caspian are more affected to unfavorable weather conditions in a sea where strong winds and storms are frequent. As a result, closures or operational restrictions for weather reasons are frequent at Caspian ports, e.g., Aktau port was closed for 53 days in 2019. Weather conditions is mentioned as one of the main reasons for irregular and unpredictable schedules found on Caspian shipping lines.

---

[15] At interviews with shipping companies, it was acknowledged that a portion of Azerbaijan and Kazakhstan fleets were deployed outside the Caspian.

[16] Data provided by AZE Government stakeholders.

5. Assessment of Multimodal Corridors

This section summarizes key findings about multimodal corridors linking landlocked CAREC countries to seaports and identifies a few issues and challenges.

5.1. Baltic Corridor (CAREC 1 and 6 b, c)

5.1.1. Rail transport

Rail transport along this corridor benefits from continuous 1,520 millimeter (mm) gauge from ports in the Russian Federation and the EU Baltic countries down to Central Asia Republics as a legacy from common former Soviet Union infrastructure. However, change of gauge is required from 1,520 mm to 1,435 mm rail track at the Poland–Belarus and Poland–Russian Federation (Kaliningrad) borders where some constraints exist.

In 2017, 12.5 million tons were transported through all Belarusian–Polish border crossings. On average, 24 trains passed through this border per day. The total capacity of all Belarusian–Polish rail border crossings was 50 pairs of freight trains per day (26 – on a gauge of 1,520 mm, 24 – 1,435 mm). The main border crossing both for freight and passenger transport is Malaszewicze–Brest. Other crossing points are Bruzhi–Kuznika and Svilach–Semianowka.

Polish railways have a modernization plan of Malaszewicze area that will enable to achieve capacity of up to 55 pairs of trains per day, both gauges. The capacity of container terminals of Polish Railways (PKP) Cargo will be also increased. Belarus Railways plans to increase the existing capacity of Brest Severny station from current 992 TEU to 1,380 TEU per day. Besides the investments in railway infrastructure mentioned above, a number of organizational improvements are necessary. For example, it is proposed to transfer part of the shunting work on the selection of containers from Brest to Kolyadichi terminal at Minsk node, and thereby reduce the operating time of containers at Brest node. Insufficiently harmonized border and customs clearance cause border crossing delays. In 2018, Russian Railways (RZD) and Belarus Railways (BCh) digitalized consignment notes of all bilateral freight traffic, as is the case on route Kaliningrad–Lithuania–Belarus–Russian Federation and in the opposite direction. Similar solution should be a standard in case of CIM/SMGS international rail freight transport. (European Commission 2019).

It takes 18–21 hours to change gauge at main crossing points between Poland and Belarus as shown in Table 3 , while it takes between 2 and 4.5 hours on Kazakhstan–PRC rail crossing points.

An additional bottleneck is that maximum train lengths are different, longer in the Russian Federation and Belarus (900 m and more), while in Poland the technical regulations limit train length to 600 m.

Table 3: Comparison Rail Crossing Points between Belarus–Poland and the People's Republic of China–Kazakhstan

	Crossing point	Max frequency of trains per day on 1,520mm	Max frequency of trains per day on 1,435mm	Terminal capacity TEU per day	Transhipment time (hrs.)
Belarus–Poland	Brest–Malaszewicze	14	15	1,590	21
	Bruzhi–Kuznika	6	4	160	8
	Svilach–Semianowka	6	5	3,000	18
Kazakhstan–PRC	Dostyk–Alashankou	12–14	6	1,400	4.5
	Altynkol–Khorgos	12–20	10	18,000	2

Source: United Transport and Logistics Company – Eurasian Rail Alliance.

Table 4: Rail Fares of United Transport and Logistics Company – Eurasian Rail Alliance

Route	Transport fare loaded 40' ($)	USD/Km
Westbound	2,700-3,000	0.52-0.58
Eastbound	2,400-2,800	0.48-0.56

The table shows the composite index ERAI that includes the cost of transit container shipments in the Eurasian Rail Corridor across Kazakhstan, Russian Federation, and Belarus between the border points with the PRC and the border points with the EU.

Source: United Transport and Logistics Company – Eurasian Rail Alliance

Russian, Belarus, and Kazakhstan railways have created UTLC Eurasian Rail Alliance as a cooperation platform to offer integrated freight forwarding services on the PRC–Europe rail corridor but also PRC–Moscow and other Russian destinations. UTLC-ERA rates for 40' container on this corridor can be followed though the application ERAI 1520 at https://index1520.com/en/. Table 4 shows the ranges of rail fares for the China-EU traffic for the past 3 years.

CIS countries plus the PRC railways use the OSJD standards and SMGS consignment note. Eastern and Central European countries that were members of the former Soviet Union also use them but have also adopted COTIF standards and CIM consignment note. A joint CIM/SMGS consignment note has been developed in paper and electronic format that allows seamless movement using a single consignment note. However, railways west of the former Soviet Union use only COTIF/CIM standards.

The Baltic corridor has relatively low importance for most Central Asia countries than other corridors, since imports from Europe, especially high-volume/low-value rail-friendly commodities are relatively small. This creates a shortage of capacity (wagons) for Central Asia exports to Europe.

5.1.2. Road Transport

Though Central Asia exports more to Europe than it imports, in fact most of exports are crude oil, gas, and other hydrocarbons that move by pipeline. Road transport costs reflect an imbalance of flows with haulage costs from West to East much higher than otherwise. Freight costs to Kazakhstan were $1.40 per km from Poland and $1.08 from Latvia. However, backhaul rates were less than half on the range of $0.45 per km.[17] As distances to Almaty, Tashkent, or Bishkek on the range of 4,500 to 5,000 km, road haulage cost for imports are on average above $5,000, but much lower for exports.

EAEU customs union and associated free movement agreements enable the development of a dynamic haulage market and reduce barriers for movements of trucks and drivers. Stakeholders consulted have mentioned that Belarus trucks and drivers and also from Baltic Countries are the most common to be found transporting cargoes from Baltic and North Europe to Central Asia. However, stakeholders also voice concerns about some hassle and corruption still prevalent in some areas.

5.1.3. SWOT Analysis

Figure 16 in SWOT format summarizes main findings for Baltic Corridor.

Figure 16: SWOT: Baltic Corridor

Strengths	Weaknesses
1. Seamless rail connectivity to Russian and Baltic ports (UTLC, 1,520 mm gauge, SMGS).	1. Transhipment times and capacity shortages at Poland/Belarus railway crossings.
2. EAEU enables the development of a dynamic road haulage market and reduce barriers for movements of trucks and drivers.	2. Hassle and corruption at some points.
	3. Long distances.

Opportunities	Threats
1. Imbalance of flows offer low trucking rates for Central Asia exports.	1. Souring EU–Russian Federation and/or EU–Belarus relations.

EAEU = Eurasian Economic Union; EU = European Union; SMGS = Agreement on International Railway Freight Communications; SWOT = Strengths, Weaknesses, Opportunities, and Threats; UTLC = United Transport and Logistics Company.

Source: Consultants.

[17] Source: DELLA. www.della.eu. Rates at end 2019.

5.2. Mediterranean and Black Sea Corridor (CAREC 2 and 6a)

5.2.1. Rail Transport

The Trans-Caucasus corridor used to be a busy route for oil and fuels in the past. However, volumes have dropped substantially after the entry into operations of several pipelines, notably the Baku–Tbilisi–Ceyhan system. This has had severe impact on the business of Azerbaijan and Georgia railways.

In this scenario railways companies from Georgia, Azerbaijan, Kazakhstan, Turkey, and Ukraine, plus the ports of Batumi, Alat, Aktau, and national shipping companies ASCO (AZE) and Kazmortransflot (Kazakhstan) have joined efforts to develop new Asia–Europe traffics across the Caspian and Black seas under the brand "Middle Corridor" through a partnership named Trans-Caspian International Transport Route (TITR, also known as TMTM from the acronym in Russian). TITR still does not provide direct freight forwarding services as UTLC-ERA does. According to TITR, the number of TEU from the PRC to the Caucasus and Turkey increased from almost none in 2017 to 15,000 in 2018 and 30,000 in 2019.

The completion of the railway line Baku–Tbilisi–Kars (BTK) in 2017 allows direct connection between Central Asia networks to Turkey across Georgia and Azerbaijan. Traffic statistics illustrate volumes growing from 130 TEU in 2017 to 4,400 in 2018,[18] but still low. The first train PRC to Europe (Prague) using this route was inaugurated on November 2019.

However, substantial infrastructure bottlenecks on the Trans-Caucasus route still exist. Typically, PRC–EU trains carry 42–44 FEU. Kazakhstan and Russian trains have usually 32 wagons with capacity for 4 TEU per wagon (total 64 FEU). However, Georgia Railways has capped capacity on block trains: to 29 wagons for 58 TEU (29 FEU) and 1,900 tons per train, because of Rikoti Pass. Moreover, Akhalkalaki pass on the Tbilisi-Kars line caps capacity to 36 TEU (18 FEU) only or 18 wagons per train. A further bottleneck is Marmaray Tunnel under the Bosphorus that was designed for passengers, and has limits for freight trains. Both Georgia and Turkey have plans to overcome these bottlenecks.

TITR is actively promoting the corridor and stakeholders acknowledge that its partners are taking commercial risks (i.e., applying reductions) in their fares. Rail tariffs on TITR routes are available on https://middlecorridor.com/en/route. Tariffs are inclusive of shipping costs across the Caspian. TITR fares per Km are comparable with those of UTLC as illustrated in the table below, though transit time is longer in spite of shorter distance. This possibly reflects among other factors the additional time required in the shunting, ferry loading and unloading and shipping across the Caspian as well as waiting times.

Table 5: Benchmark Fares of the Trans-Caspian International Transport Route and United Transport and Logistics Company

	Route	Kilometer	Fare 40' ($)	$/kilometer	Time
TITR	Altynkol–Poti	4,500	2,435	0.54	10 days
	Poti–Altynkol	4,500	1,888	0.42	10 days
	Altynkol–Aktau–Absheron (Baku)	3,721	2,207	0.59	8 days
	Absheron (Baku)–Aktau–Altynkol	3,721	1,660	0.45	8 days
UTLC	Altynkol–Brest	5,200	2,700–3,000	0.52–0.58	6 days
	Brest–Altynkol	5,200	2,400–2,800	0.48–0.56	6 days

Source: Trans-Caspian International Transport Route website https://middlecorridor.com/en, against United Transport and Logistics Company- Eurasian Rail Alliance.

---

[18] Data provided by Georgia Railways.

Rail infrastructure at Poti Port.

Neither Poti nor Batumi ports have efficient rail connection down to the dockside container terminals (see sections on Poti and Batumi ports in Volume II). In the case of Batumi, it is space-constrained and needs complex shunting. In the case of Poti rail connection for breakbulk is available at the dockside but the rail container terminal is located about 3 Km away so that a truck shuttle is necessary.

Recent research (KPMG Georgia LLC, Dec, 2019) has concluded that the combination of the Middle Corridor and Black Sea ferries may be an attractive option for cargoes between Central Asia and the coastal nations around the Black Sea (Turkey, Bulgaria, Romania, and Ukraine), plus Greece; but hardly beyond, where the UTLC northern corridor is more competitive. Other studies also mention that this route is unlikely to compete with other routes to link with Northern and Central Europe's industrial heartlands. (Kenderdine, expected 2021)

However, it is to be noted that the Middle Corridor is an essential lifeline for some major industrial complexes located far inland in Central Asia such as fertilizers plant in Mary (Turkmenistan) and TALCO aluminium plant in Tursunzade (Tajikistan). However, others such as Uz-Kor Chemicals in Nukus (Uzbekistan) that exports polymers to the port of Mersin avoid the trans-Caspian route and instead cargoes are moved by truck across Kazakhstan, the Russian Federation, Azerbaijan, Georgia, and Turkey.[19]

---

[19] In the first case, export of urea is a booming business that has led to expansion plans for breakbulk storage facilities both at Poti and Batumi ports. In the second case, alumina is imported from Europe and other origins to Tajikistan and aluminum ingots exported. This is also a substantial business across the Caspian and at Poti port. In the third case, it was mentioned that they benefited from cheap backhaul transport rates from Turkish truck companies.

Box 7: Tariffs and Incentives on the Trans-Caspian International Transport Route Corridor

The Trans-Caspian International Transport Route (TITR) tariffs mentioned in Table 5 include shipping across the Caspian using a rail ferry. The amount of subsidy is unknown. However, an indication of its magnitude can be derived from the following calculations:

According to Azerbaijan Caspian Shipping Company (ASCO) published tariffs, the cost of shipping a container from Alat port to Aktau is $1,200. No published fare is available for Kazmortransflot.

If we considered that ASCO was not discounting its fare in the operation, the ferry fare would represent between 49% to 72% of the TITR integrated multimodal fare. In this case the residual revenue per Km of railways would be too low to become feasible.

Ferry and Rail Contribution to Middle Corridor Fares

Item	Fare	Caspian Ferry as Total of Fare (%)	Residual Rail Revenue per kilometer
Altynkol-Poti/Batumi	2,435	49.28	0.27
Poti/Batumi-Altynkol	1,888	63.56	0.15
Altinkol-Aktau-Absheron (Baku)	2,207	54.37	0.27
Absheron (Baku)-Aktau-Altynkol	1,660	72.29	0.12

It is also interesting to note that Georgia Railways published 2019 tariff for 1 FEU Poti to Baku was $1,000. This a quite expensive rate for the 900 kilometer (km) journey ($1.1/km).

It is not known how TITR costs are shared by railways companies of the various countries, shipping companies and port operators, being all of them government-owned or controlled state-owned enterprises (SOEs). Indeed, in Kazakhstan, the Railways KTZ controls Kuryk Port where the rail ferries call. On the Azerbaijani side, Port of Baku and ASCO, the only shipping company providing rail ferries across the Caspian,[a] are also government-owned, but independent companies from Azerbaijan Railways (ADY).

Similarly, it is not transparent how costs are shared for longer journeys across the Black Sea e.g., Altynkol–Constanta ($3,535 westbound; $2,998 eastbound). Most TITR traffic seems to be directed through Batumi port where another Kazakhstan SOE is managing the port. However since ferry charges across the Black Sea are between $900 to $1,200 (KPMG Georgia LLC Dec 2019), it does not seem that shipping companies (mostly private) are offering substantial discounts.

[a] This was the situation at the beginning of 2020.

Source: TITR, ASCO, Georgia Rail, KPMG Georgia; LLC, Dec, 2019 and Authors' calculations.

5.2.2. Road Transport

Georgia and Azerbaijan's international road transport sector is small, about 300 medium-sized TIR operators in Georgia and about 100 in Azerbaijan.[20] Georgia has harmonized trucking standards according to EU regulations. Technical barriers with Azerbaijan seem not to be an issue.

The Mediterranean-Black Sea corridor by road faces two major challenges:

1. Still Unresolved Road Bottlenecks and Gaps

Though both Georgia and Azerbaijan have substantially upgraded road infrastructure on the East–West corridor, it is not up to full motorway standards except in very

---

[20] Source: GIRCA and ABADA.

few sections and is still single carriage or two lanes in some sections with no short-term plans for upgrading. Moreover, both Georgia and Azerbaijan have been hesitant at implementing toll road schemes in their upgraded roads, thus limiting their financial capacity to invest and/or maintain new infrastructure. The situation at the end of 2019 in the East–West road corridor was:

(i)   M2 road from Alat port west to Ganja is dual carriageway and four lanes, though not offering proper motorway standards since the road is not insulated from surroundings and runs across most urban settlements on its way.
(ii)   From Ganja to the Red Bridge (border with Georgia) it is for the most part a single carriageway, two lanes road. The Government of Azerbaijan has upgrading project in the pipeline.
(iii)   From the Red Bridge to Rustavi the road is single carriageway, two lanes.
(iv)   From Rustavi to Tbilisi it is a dual carriageway standard motorway.
(v)   From Tbilisi to Kutaisi several works to upgrade the whole corridor to motorway standards are under way, including a new tunnel at Rikoti pass.
(vi)   From Kutaisi to Poti and Batumi, the road reverts to single carriageway, two lanes and no short nor medium term project to upgrade it exists.

Across the Caspian, west Kazakhstan is a very sparsely populated area that attracts and generates few cargoes except project cargo bound to the oilfields.

On the way from Aktau to Almaty there is no road shortcut from Beyneu to Ayteke Bi, while it exists for rail, obliging an almost 1,000 km detour.

2. Unresolved Inefficiencies to Cross the Caspian

Excessive and uncertain waiting times at Caspian Ports is a repeated concern of private sector stakeholders. Waiting times seem not to be such an issue on the Kazakhstan side of the Caspian. Caspian ferries are designed for rail wagons but can also accommodate trucks though apparently rail wagons take priority. In addition, the Caspian is prone to strong winds and bad weather that restricts shipping operations. During the site visit, consultants could observe about 100 trucks waiting within Alat port premises. Also, it was confirmed that no published schedule of ferries was available so that trips could be planned in advance, though port authorities and shipping companies were working to fix a regular schedule. See more on caps and restrictions on Caspian shipping in section 4.5.

The Russian route to avoid the Caspian has also some drawbacks, one of them being administrative hassle and informal payments. Some stakeholders mentioned that the decision to cross the Caspian on ferry or by-pass it across the Russian Federation highly depended on the value and type of cargo. Drivers felt safer moving valuable or time sensitive cargoes by ferry than driving across the Russian Federation. Also, some cargoes such as meat find restrictions to move

Dual carriageway road near Baku without the proper motorway standards.

across the Russian Federation. However, this route seemed to be used for empty backhauls. Another complaint referred to the Russian Federation's e-tolls system (Platon). Levy in 2019 was RUB2.20 per km ($0.034) for trucks over 12 tons. The system requires drivers to buy or rent an on-board unit (OBU) per truck to process e-payments.

Another issue mentioned by stakeholders in both Georgia and Azerbaijan and other countries in the region is the visa regime for drivers in Turkmenistan. Despite various agreements signed, in particular, between Turkmenistan and Azerbaijan, this seems still to be an unresolved issue.

International road transport rates at the end of 2019 were in the range of $1 to $1.3 per km on the routes west to east and around 0.70 east to west.[21] Haulage companies in Azerbaijan, Georgia, and Kazakhstan complain about competition from Turkish trucks loaded with exports from Turkey and offering very cheap rates for backhaul cargo.

5.2.3. Logistics Centers

Neither Georgia nor Azerbaijan have sizeable logistics centers offering Class-A warehouses[22] and rail container terminals are small in size and volumes handled. In view of overcoming this weakness, both

Table 6: Plans for Logistics Centers and Free Zones in Georgia and Azerbaijan

	Project	Promoter	Surface (hectare)	Vocation	Status
Georgia	Poti Free Industrial Zone	Public–Private	300	Industrial Logistics	Incipient development
	Anaklia Port	Private	2,000 (initial stage 400)	Industrial Logistics Financial Tourism	On hold
	Kutaisi Airport Logistics Centre	Government	39	Regional distribution Airfreight Container terminal	Feasibility studies completed
	Kumisi Logistics Centre	Government	43	National distribution Container terminal	Feasibility studies completed
Azerbaijan	Alat Port Free Zone	Government	100	Truck Parking International Logistics Centre Domestic Logistic Centre	PIU set up to launch first phase in 2020
	Absheron Logistics center	Private	65	Rail to road facilities Warehousing	Incipient development

Sources: https://potifreezone.ge; http://anakliadevelopment.com; (Dornier Consulting, 2017); https://portofbaku.com; http://www.absheronport.az.

---

[21] Source: www.della.eu.

[22] Classification of warehouses into categories A, B, and C is widely used in the real estate industry specialized in logistics, although there are no international standards setting the technical specifications for these categories. Guidelines set by various organizations are available. For informative purposes, the main criteria used in France (Source: https://www.eol.fr/article-805-la-classification-des-entrepots.html) are: *Class A*: (i) Height over 9.3 meters; (ii) Manoeuvring area deeper than 35 meters; (iii) One dock per 1,000 square meters (m²); (iv) Ground resistance greater than 5 tons/m² and (v) Heating and fire extinguishing system. *Class B*: (i) Height over 7.5 meters; (ii) Manoeuvring area deeper than 32 meters; (iii) One dock per 1,500 m²; (iv) Ground resistance greater than 3 tons per m² and (v) Fire extinguishing system. *Class C*: those below A or B standards.

countries have schemes to promote logistics areas and free zones. Most identified projects are either on early stages of development or not yet launched, as is illustrated in Table 6. The apparent little appetite of private sector to invest in some government sponsored logistics parks may reflect concerns about their size, location or proposed business model.

5.2.4. Containerization

Though most cargo from the PRC to Central Asia is containerized and moves by rail, most nonbulk cargo from Europe and Turkey to Central Asia moves by truck. Movement of TEU by Georgia Railways, around 70,000 in 2019, is only half the number of TEU handled in Altynkol only on the same year. Most container trains at Poti or Batumi head to Tbilisi, Yerevan or Baku and very few containers travel beyond Azerbaijan into Central Asia. Indeed, the last available figure for container throughput in Aktau was 14,300 TEU, in Alat was 35,100 and in Turkmenbashi was about 19,000. It is not possible to discern how many of them were owned by shippers or by shipping lines.

Most stakeholders consulted have stated that shipping lines are reluctant to allow containers inland beyond Baku and that usual practice in Poti and Batumi ports is destuffing containers and loading into wagons or tarpaulin trucks for onward transport.

A rationale for transhipping heavy and low value commodities from containers to rail wagons exist when transport cost per ton/km is critical, as (i) more tonnage can be loaded on rail wagons (up to 60 tons) than in trucks (max payload about 22 tons); (ii) payload does not include the tare of containers (2.2 tons per TEU, 3.7 tons per FEU); and (iii) economies of transport cost per ton/km offset additional handling and transhipping costs.

However, moving containers on rail in distances in the range of 900–1,000 km as is the case of Poti/Batumi to Baku/Alat is being preconized under efficiency and environmental considerations in most gateway ports. Further investigation on logistics practice on the Black Sea–Caspian route could identify where barriers and impediments exist, how could they be lifted and offer opportunities for more efficient intermodal flows.

Box 8: Costs of Non-Containerization Poti to Baku

Stakeholders mention few containers move from Georgia's Black Sea ports inland to Baku and beyond.

The cost of moving a 40' container is $1,000 by rail according to tariffs of Georgia Railways for 2019. This rate is relatively high compared to other corridors (more than $1/km).

Cost of a trailer truck on the same route is $1,200. The cost of destuffing a container in Poti and loading onto a truck is estimated to be between $150 and $250 if cargo is palletized and up to $500 if not palletized[a]. Assuming that all the stuff inside the container can be loaded into a single truck, cost will go up to $1,350 in the best case to $1,700 in the worst.

[a] Stakeholder interviews at Poti Port.
Source: Stakeholders interviews at Poti Port.

It is therefore key for the Middle Corridor to improve the commercial, technical, and physical capabilities to handle container traffic in a competitive manner.

5.2.5. SWOT Analysis

Figure 17 in SWOT format summarizes the main findings for Mediterranean and Black Sea Corridor.

5.3. Arabian Sea - Iran Corridor (CAREC 3a, b and 6a, b)

5.3.1. Rail Transport

Iran provides the shortest route to deep seaports for Turkmenistan, Uzbekistan, and Afghanistan. Iran railway network connects with Turkey, Turkmenistan, and Pakistan but there is a missing link to connect with Azerbaijan's main network.[23]

The Sarakhs/Saraks and the Akyayla/Incheboroun are the two main international railway border crossings between Iran and Turkmenistan. The Srakhs/Saraks border crossing, that became operational in 1996, is the main railway link

---

[23] Russian Railways (RZD) has launched a multimodal service from Mumbai Nhava Sheva port to Europe through Bandar Abbas and across Azerbaijan.

Figure 17: SWOT: Mediterranean and Black Sea Corridor

Strengths	Weaknesses
1. Marketing and promotion platform (Trans-Caspian International Transport Route/TMTM) operational.	1. Corridor is attractive for a limited cluster of countries in South-Eastern Europe and Turkey.
2. Upgraded Caspian ports infrastructure.	2. Unresolved inefficiencies to cross the Caspian.
3. BTK link with Turkey and Europe.	3. A typical Central Asia-European Union (EU) shipment will involve moving across four customs territories, instead of two if using a route across Eurasian Economic Union.
	4. Bottlenecks and gaps both on Trans-Caucasus rail and road infrastructure.
	5. Little use of containers on the corridor.
	6. Unresolved capacity and rail access issues at Georgian ports.

Opportunities	Threats
1. Openness of Caucasus countries and alignment with EU standards.	1. The attractiveness of the corridor, underpinned by incentives may dilute when they are removed.
2. Most infrastructure bottlenecks are identified and projects are on the pipeline.	2. Investment decisions diverted to lesser productive projects.
3. Kanal Istanbul may eventually open new opportunities for Black Sea ports	3. Improved corridor Tehran–Istanbul and lifting of sanctions on Iran.

SWOT = Strengths, Weaknesses, Opportunities, and Threats.

Source: Consultants.

between CIS countries and Iran and the main access to the Iranian ports at the Persian Gulf. Before sanctions, around 85% of the rail transit across Islamic Republic of Iran was handled over Sarakhs border station.[24]

A change of bogie systems organized in both countries is the principal way of dealing with break of gauge from 1,435 mm in Iran to 1,520 in Turkmenistan. The capacity for change of bogies in both countries is not balanced being less in Turkmenistan. Moreover, no infrastructure for container transhipment is available at the border, thus little containerized cargo crosses the border.

Towards Afghanistan, the rail link from Khaf (Iran) to Herat (Afghanistan) is being completed. Connection from Iran through Turkmenistan would also be theoretically possible via the cross border link at Serhetabat (Turkmenistan) to Torghundi (Afghanistan) and a new rail line Atamyrat

(Turkmenistan) in Turkmenistan to Akina opened in 2016, eventually linking with Uzbekistan and Tajikistan. However, moving across Turkmenistan means gauge change at the border. Moving cargoes by train from Iran to Afghanistan and onwards will become more attractive once rail line to Herat is completed.

Despite the existing gap between Iran and Azerbaijan networks, Russian Railways (RZD) has launched a multimodal service from Mumbai Nhava Sheva port to Europe through Bandar Abbas and across Azerbaijan.

Before the imposition of sanctions,[25] Bandar Abbas used to be the preferred gateway port for Uzbekistan. Nowadays the use of Iranian ports for most Central Asian cargoes has greatly decreased with the exception is Afghanistan that is actively using Iran ports, in particular Chabahar, that benefits from some exemptions to United States (US) sanctions.

---

[24] Source: UNESCAP 2018.

[25] Iran is the subject of a variety of sanctions imposed by the US, the EU, and other countries. As a result, most international shipping lines avoid calling at Iranian ports and a substantial share of trade is done by Iran flag feeder ships calling at major hubs, notably Jebel Ali in the UAE (see Volume II). Another substantial hurdle to business with Iran is the removal from the SWIFT international payment system.

Figure 18: SWOT: Arabian Sea - Iran Corridor

Strengths	Weaknesses
1. Shortest route from Arabian Sea ports into Central Asia. 2. Relatively well performing rail and road transport.	1. Sanctions to Iran are drastically limiting the use of the corridor. 2. Turkmenistan/Iran rail border crossing not having facilities for container transhipment and limited capacity. 3. Missing rail link with Azerbaijan.
Opportunities	Threats
1. Lifting of sanctions may put Iran again as a central player for trade to/from Central Asia 2. Bottlenecks and inefficiencies are shifting transit trade to Afghanistan from Pakistan to Iran 3. Chabahar port, less impacted by sanctions, developing as major gateway to Afghanistan.	1. Conflict and instability in the Arabian Gulf. 2. Long-term duration of sanctions further eroding Iran's economy and impacting fleet renewal, infrastructure upgrades, and maintenance, etc.

SWOT = Strengths, Weaknesses, Opportunities, and Threats.

Source: Consultants.

5.3.2. Road Transport

Despite sanctions, some companies in landlocked Central Asian countries are still using tuck transport for imports and exports through Bandar Abbas. Transport costs are on the range of $1 to $1.20/km, not far away of standard costs in other Central Asia corridors, though it is to be noted that Iran haulage companies benefit from one of the cheapest diesel prices in the world at $0.02 per liter.

Foreign transport companies mention that quotas and road charges penalize them in Iran. Adding road charges to haulage tariffs make them out of market. On the contrary, Iran truckers are active outside their country into Kazakhstan and even into the Russian Federation. Iranian trucks are also common along Azerbaijan's North–South corridor bound to Baku or transiting to the Russian Federation.

5.3.3. SWOT analysis

Figure 18 in SWOT format summarizes the main findings for Arabian Sea-Iran corridor.

5.4.　Arabian Sea - Pakistan (CAREC 5 and 6)

5.4.1. Rail Transport

The main freight corridor of Pakistan Railways (PR) is ML1 that runs 1,872 km from Karachi to Lahore, Islamabad, and Peshawar. The line from Karachi to Lahore is double track, with a design speed of 120 kilometers per hour (kph) (freight) and 23 tonne axle load capability. Beyond Lahore the line is single track with 95 kph design speeds and 23 tonne axle load capacity. Most of the rest of the network is 95 kph, with 23 tonne axle loads; some branch lines have lower speeds and 18 tonne axle load capability.

ML2 is also north–south on the west of ML1 but currently not operational.

ML3 runs west from Rohri to Quetta where it splits with one branch to Chaman on the Afghan border and another to Taftan on the Iran border. Its use for cargoes is very limited.

Railway freight market share was about 5% (based on tonne-kilometres) until rail freight transport nearly collapsed in 2011/12. Recent increases in rail freight traffic have lifted rail market share to about 2%, being coal and petroleum products the main commodities transported (Ministry of Railways & Pakistan Railways, 2019).

Most container trains head to various Inland Container Terminals (ICT) located near Lahore in a journey that typically lasts 24 hrs. On average, traffic is one container train per day from Karachi Ports and two or three from Qasim.

Typical train length is 30 wagons with capacity for 60 TEU. However, current maximum acceptable payload per train is 1,000 tons at ML1 and 800 tons at ML2.

There are plans to increase acceptable payload up to 2,400 tons, i.e. 40 wagons with 60 tons payload.[26]

Rail is little used for transit trade to Afghanistan. One of the reasons is that most traffic bound for Afghanistan is discharged in Karachi ports not in Qasim, that have less good rail connections, as is discussed later.

Poor performance and limited standards of service reduce the attractiveness of rail to shippers. It is to note also than according to consulted stakeholders, one of the reasons hampering the development of rail freight market is poor enforcement of limits on maximum load for road transport.[27]

Of the three container terminals in Karachi Port only one, PICT, has direct operational railway access as also has Qasim port. There are infrastructure gaps (around 3.7 km) to connect KICT terminal directly to the rail. Regarding SAPT terminal, rail connection is envisaged only in phase 2 though PR is pushing the terminal operator to build it earlier.

To overcome the difficulties and restrictions across the city for port-bound trucks[28] PR has proposed a series of actions. One of them is to move containers by rail from Karachi and Qasim port terminals to a marshalling yard at Pipri where PR owns of 2,000 acres (around 800 ha) of land available for rail as well as for logistics and industrial development. They plan that containers would be shuttled from port terminals by rail to Pipri where they would either continue by rail upcountry or be transhipped to trucks to distribution in Karachi area and shorter distances. The ambition is that the project could be developed on a build–operate–transfer (BOT) scheme. The operation is inspired in the Alameda Corridor in Los Angeles. Various port and private sector stakeholders expressed doubts to the consultants about the wisdom of this project for a variety of reasons— existing poor rail infrastructure across Karachi, and unresolved gaps and encroachments, and too short distance, in particular from Qasim, to make shuttle trains and transhipment an economic option.

Rail infrastructure in Karachi, Pakistan.

---

[26] Source: Interview with Ministry of Railways.

[27] At the time of the consultants visit in January 2020, road haulage sector had taken industrial action against government introduction of more severe controls on load compliance. According to some stakeholders, when controls were stricter, use of rail increased.

[28] Karachi Municipal Corporation has restricted circulation of trucks at some access roads to the port terminals during daytime, however at the time of the site visit compliance was far from general.

PR liberalized and offered rail access to private operators in 2011. However, according to private stakeholders interviewed, there are still too many undefined legal areas that have shun private operators away (e.g., responsibilities in case of damage caused by track condition). PR is currently working on the implementation of the Pakistan Railways Strategic Plan to revamp its business.

Under the CPEC initiative PR envisages to upgrade ML1 as follows:[29]

(i)   From current capacity of 34 trains per day (pax + cargo) up to 170 trains per day
(ii)   From current capacity of trains of 1,000 tons payload to up to 2,400 tons payload per train (40 wagons with 60 tons payload).
(iii)   From current axle load per wagon of 22 tons up to 25.

However, no final agreement on the financing had been reached at the time of drafting this report as of February 2020.

Other Government plans are:

(i)   For ML3, a feasibility study has been done to redevelop the line under BOT. Current maximum payload per train is 800 tons.
(ii)   Extension of railway from Peshawar to Jalalabad (Afghanistan)
(iii)   A new railway line linking Quetta with Gwadar Port and onwards to Herat in Afghanistan is envisaged. It will include railways and container yards at Gwadar. Feasibility studies are completed, land acquisition started and budget for some sections allocated.

5.4.2. Road Transport

Road network in Pakistan shows a variety of situations. Toll motorways are being deployed along main axes featuring good standards of service. However, truck drivers often avoid using them and keep using the nontolled alternative roads, causing undesired damage.

Road transport fleet in Pakistan is mostly obsolete and noncompliant to international standards. Overloading is a structural practice and the government faces unsurmountable opposition to strict compliance.

Most transit trade from Pakistan ports head to Afghanistan with little moving further to Tajikistan and other Central Asia countries or to the PRC.

Pakistan is signatory of TIR Convention as well as Afghanistan, Tajikistan, and the PRC, thus in theory this should facilitate transit. However, TIR in Pakistan was only activated in 2018 and thus still in early implementation. Moreover, various barriers make it difficult a seamless movement of cargoes.

Though the Afghan-Pakistan Transit Trade Agreement (APTTA) has been operational since 2011. From its beginnings, there have been issues involving the processes such as excessive dwell time, delays at the port of entry, cost burdens involving financial guarantees for transit trucks, monopoly trucking by licensing limited numbers of bonded carriers or insurance guarantees for freight. Despite TIR, as a rule of thumb Pakistan plated trucks won't drive beyond Jalalabad and Afghanistan trucks will not go beyond Peshawar. Transit cargo is subject to jealous monitoring as pilfering and smuggling is a major problem. Thus both countries have made efforts on tight security protocols for the transit route to avoid containers in transit being stolen or pilfered.

Improvement projects at main BCP with Afghanistan at Torkham, Chaman with funding support from ADB are under way. Also, improvements are planned at the BCP with India at Wagah.

Transit cargoes to Tajikistan across Afghanistan are affected by additional issues:

(i)   Pakistan Customs IT system is not accepting for the moment declarations with Tajikistan as the final destination, even though trade agreements allow it. This obliges to double declarations, first to Afghanistan, and then to Tajikistan.
(ii)   Difficulties for Afghan drivers to obtain Tajikistan visa. Drivers from Tajikistan and other central Asia countries are unwilling to drive in Afghanistan.
(iii)   Security and informal payments are a prevalent issue in Afghanistan.

---

[29] From meeting with Directorate General, Planning at Ministry of Railways, Pakistan.

Transit cargoes from Karachi ports to Central Asia (the Kyrgyz Republic or Kazakhstan) through the PRC are theoretically possible and in terms of transit time attractive compared with moving cargo from Pacific ports. However, stakeholders consulted mention formidable challenges beyond those associated with weather and road conditions across the Khunjerab pass, i.e., long waiting times, exhaustive security controls, need to tranship cargoes to Chinese trucks at Kashgar and again in the Kyrgyz Republic or Kazakhstan. Only a few entrepreneurs are actively using this route. It is hoped that full implementation of TIR procedures will facilitate moving cargoes along this route.

Road transport costs for transit cargoes to Afghanistan and beyond appear to be higher than domestic cargoes on PAK North–South corridor or in other corridors analyzed in this study.

5.4.3. Containerization

Containers are moved by rail and road upcountry from Karachi and Qasim ports to Lahore, where several dry ports exist and to lesser extent up to Islamabad and Peshawar. So that to promote rail transit trade to Khyber–Pakhtunkhwa and onwards to Afghanistan a new dry port at Azakhel was inaugurated in January 2020. It is spread over 28 acres and located about 20 km east from Peshawar. A dry port near Havelian will also be constructed.

Following the transit agreement, 100% transit to Afghanistan are sealed containers. But concerns about loss and delayed return of transit containers on the Pakistan–Afghanistan route have been prevalent. Though some consulted stakeholders acknowledged

improvements in container turnaround time making the 14 days grace period an attainable target, the high upfront costs either for deposits or for the acquisition of nonrefundable containers are systematically adding a burden to transit trade to Afghanistan.

Box 9: Extra Costs for Unreliable Logistics: Karachi to Kabul

Typically shipping lines allow 14 days grace time for import containers before charging a penalty fee for detention. Afghanistan traders are lobbying so far unsuccessfully for a longer grace period. Usual penalty fee for detention is $95–$100 per day and a deposit of $2,000 per 20-foot equivalent unit or $4,000 per forty-foot equivalent unit has to be paid in advance to shipping line.

To avoid this quite often shippers use nonrefundable containers. The cost of a second-hand container is estimated at $1,000–$1,200 for a twenty-foot box and $2,000 for a 40-foot box.

The cost of moving a forty-foot container by truck Karachi to Kabul is between $2,800 and $3,800, not including customs, nor duties, nor terminal handling.

If the container is not brought back to the port, the importer will forfeit the deposit guarantee of $2,000–$4,000 for failing to return the container. If the shipper uses a nonrefundable second-hand box, $2,000 will be added to the cost of transportation, i.e., about 50%–70% extra costs.

Source: Consultants interviews with stakeholders during site visits.

Table 7: Transport Costs for Transit Pakistan and Afghanistan

Route	Transport fare loaded 40'	$/kilometer	Sources
Karachi–Dushanbe	4,500–5,000	1.87–2.08	Stakeholders interviews
Karachi–Lahore	1,200–1,800	1–1.5	PIFFA
Karachi–Bishkek	7,000	1.9	PIFFA
Karachi–Kabul	2,800–3,800	1.7–2.3	PIFFA
Karachi–Kandahar	3,500	3.67	CPMM 2018
Islamabad–Almaty	6,000–6,500	2.4–2.6	Stakeholders interviews
Kabul–Almaty	4,200	2.10	Stakeholders interviews

CPMM = Corridor Performance Measurement and Monitoring, PIFFA = Pakistan International Freight Forwarding Association.
Source: CPMM 2018, PIFFA, and stakeholders interviews.

5.4.4. Logistics

The Pakistan logistics landscape is dual. On one side many international players are present, in particular in port terminals, bringing international operational standards and procedures. Good logistics capabilities and cosmopolitanism are also found among senior staff and professionals exposed to international trade, not to mention many courageous entrepreneurs.

However, skills and practice worsen as one descends to operational levels as well as among the universe of small and microenterprises focused to the domestic market.

As described in the Ports section, a myriad of vested interests, turfs, and inertias at government, private sector, trade unions, and professional corporations are slowing or directly hijacking much needed reforms.

The government seems to be aware of the situation and a National Freight and Logistics Sector Strategy has been elaborated. It is hoped that this strategy will succeed in aligning the visions and interests of many parties so that the many challenges are overcome.

5.4.5. SWOT analysis

Figure 19 in SWOT format summarizes main findings in Arabian Sea-Pakistan corridor.

5.5.   Pacific - Trans–PRC (CAREC 1, 2, 5)

5.5.1. Rail Transport

The main PRC gateway ports into Central Asia are Lianyungang and to lesser extent Tianjin. In 2014 the Government of Kazakhstan signed an agreement with Lianyungang authorities to open a rail terminal within the seaport precinct aimed at handling and transhipment of Kazakhstan's transit goods, both imports and exports. A joint venture between Lianyungang port and the Kazakhstan national railway was stablished and the port set aside an area for a container yard of 22 ha with an estimated annual capacity of 410,000 TEU, (Pierce, 2014).

From Chinese ports the main rail corridor to Central Asia and Europe runs through Chi'an and Urumqi. From there the line splits heading to two crossing

Figure 19: SWOT: Arabian Sea - Pakistan Corridor

Strengths	Weaknesses
1. Good logistics capabilities and cosmopolitanism in companies and professionals exposed to international trade. 2. Presence of major international players in the market, especially in port terminals, providing well-structured procedures. 3. Improved road infrastructure in many corridors. 4. A National Freight and Logistics Sector Policy has been finalized	1. Strong inertias at all levels (government, vested interests, industry lobbies and unions) are delaying much needed reforms. 2. Underperforming railways because of many factors (poor infrastructure, shortage of rolling stock and obsolescence, governance). 3. Obsolescence of road transport fleet, noncompliance to international standards. 4. High costs, delays, and limited reliability for transit trade to Afghanistan. 5. Hurdles of different type make transit trade to Central Asia across Afghanistan or the People's Republic of China (PRC) still too complicated.
Opportunities	**Threats**
1. Improved regional cooperation framework facilitate north–south and east–west trade flows. 2. Political stability and security in Afghanistan favor trade routes into Central Asia. 3. Full implementation of the International Road Transports Convention practice in Afghanistan, Pakistan, and the PRC.	1. Regional and domestic instability and security 2. Afghanistan transit trade shifting to Iran. 3. Country indebtedness and allocation of public resources to high profile but less productive projects.

SWOT = Strengths, Weaknesses, Opportunities, and Threats.

Source: Consultants.

points with Kazakhstan: Alashankou–Dostyk and Khorgos–Altynkol. This forms part of CR Express West routes. A separate branch leads south to Kashgar but no rail connection to the Kyrgyz Republic, Tajikistan, or Pakistan exists so far. A new railway linking Uzbekistan–the Kyrgyz Republic–the PRC through Kashgar has been discussed for years and forms one of CAREC's designated rail corridors.[30] Unfortunately, no agreed decision among involved governments about the routing (North or South route) has been reached so far. The nature of the geography makes this project a substantial engineering and financial challenge. Rail connections to Pakistan, Tajikistan, and Afghanistan are also listed as CAREC rail corridors. For its part a branch starting from Jining South goes north to Mongolia through the Erenhot–Zamyn Uud crossing point.

It is to note that a substantial share of container trains from the PRC to Central Asia and Europe do not originate at Pacific ports but at industrial and commercial clusters in inland PRC such as Chongqing, Chengdu, and Yiwu.

Since China Rail runs on standard 1,435mm gauge while both Kazakhstan and Mongolia use 1,520mm, change of gauge facilities exist at all the above-mentioned crossing points. The PRC and CIS countries are members of OSJD and apply SMGS consignment note for international freight that facilitates communications procedures across borders.

China Railways is developing intermodal transport in recent years, in particular East–West corridors, in part to compensate the decline in other domestic traffic such as coal. This said, some challenges and bottlenecks still exist within the PRC that may hamper further development of rail traffic to Central Asia and beyond. Some of these challenges are: few intermodal hubs, poor rail connections at some ports, and undeveloped containerized rail systems, all these compared with the size and ambitions about East–West multimodal rail routes. In addition, some parts of the network face congestion issues as well as poor infrastructure, in particular, at Central and West provinces. (Bucsky P., 2020)

Dostyk–Alashankou

Dostyk–Alashankou crossing point has been open since July 1991 and the movement of international rail freight transport started in 1992. It provides facilities for bogie exchange, bulk transloading, and container transhipment.

The number of container block trains has substantially increased from 14 per year in 2011 to average 14 trains per day in 2019. A substantial part of this traffic consists of PRC–Europe trains. Average time to axle change is 4.5 hours. Transshipment capacity in Dostyk is 760 TEU per day or about 275,000 per annum. (see http://kdts.kz/en/company/services/dostyk/.)

Though the new complex Khorgos–Altynkol opened in 2016, Dostyk–Alashankou remains the busiest rail crossing point between the PRC and Kazakhstan as it still handles much noncontainerized cargo.

Khorgos–Altynkol

Khorgos–Altynkol complex lies at the trans-national Special Economic Zone (SEZ) that extends at both sides of the border. While the PRC side has developed quickly, on the Kazakh side, the Eastern Gate Special Economic Zone is still in early stages of development.

The main station in Khorgos (PRC side) comprises two shunting yards, various industrial and maintenance areas, and two transhipment yards for containers with gantry cranes and one for change of bogies. There is room to accommodate additional transhipment modules in the future.

On the Kazakhstan side the complex consists of Altynkol station covering 200+ ha and 7 km long including shunting areas. There is currently one terminal for container transhipment in Altynkol and other facilities for transhipment of bulk and other cargoes.

A spur from Altynkol leads to Khorgos Eastern Gate Dry Port about 7.5 km away, which is located within the precinct to the SEZ. The Dry Port has another container transhipment terminal with daily capacity to handle 1,200–1,400 TEU and a container depot with capacity for 18,000 TEU. Thus, Altynkol has capacity to handle more than 500,000 TEU with the existing infrastructure.

The complex currently handles an average of 12–15 trains per day from the PRC and 6–8 from Kazakhstan. Total throughput on Kazakhstan side was 2.7 million tons in 2019 and 140,000 TEU. Target for 2020 is to handle 5 million tons.

---

[30] See CAREC Designated Railways corridors at https://www.carecprogram.org/?page_id=6798.

Rail transshipment operations at Khorgos gateway terminal.

The breakdown of incoming traffic handled at Altynkol in 2019 was: 52% bound to Central Asia countries, 39.5% in transit to Europe (using the Kazakhstan–Russian Federation route), 3.1% bound to the Arabian Sea (i.e., Iran), 2.7% bound to the "Middle Corridor" across the Caspian, 1.5% bound to the Russian Federation and 1.2 bound to Afghanistan.[31]

Erenhot–Zamyn Uud

For its part the Erenhot–Zamyn Uud complex is the only rail link between the PRC and Mongolia. Volumes across the border grew in last several years up to 16.7 million tons in 2016. Capacity at Zamyn Uud is 420 wagons per day.

In addition to rail-to-rail transfers, rail-to-road trans-shipments are second major activity at the Erenhot–Zamyn Uud border crossing as a substantial share of cargo is transhipped into trucks to continue to other destinations near the border or even up to Ulaanbaatar 700 km away (UNESCAP, 2018); CPMM 2018).

Official rail freight rates are not always transparent. They appear to be customized in favor of operators moving high volumes and long distances, e.g., PRC–Europe. Moreover, it is known that the PRC–Europe rail is subsidized by various entities from the PRC. Different studies estimate that subsidies may account for up to 50% of transport costs on the PRC side. (EDB 2019), (Bucsky P. 2020). Central PRC authorities have announced willingness to progressively reduce discounts and eventually remove them once demand is consolidated and performance and transit time can be further reduced, though subsidies may be maintained by provincial and other subnational entities.

5.5.2. Road Transport

Uzbekistan and Kazakhstan are the major players in this corridor for international road transport. Harmonized standards according to Minsk Convention 1999 apply, though Kazakhstan requested an exemption limiting maximum gross weight (MGW) for 5 axle trailers to 36 tons. Moreover, members from the EAEU customs union benefit from the removal of transport quotas, though cabotage is not allowed yet.

---

[31] Source: KTZ Altynkol Station.

Box 10: Border Crossing Time Beyond Transhipment Between Gauges

Despite improved facilities that have reduced the time needed for transhipment between different gauge, the overall times required to cross the border remain very high as illustrated below.

Gauge transhipment against total border crossing time

Hours needed for transhipment between gauges (container traffic)	Hours needed to cross border according to CPMM18	
Dostyk–Alashankou: 4.5	Dostyk inbound: 61.0	Alashankou outbound: 21.9
	Dostyk outbound: n.a.	Alashankou inbound: n.a.
Khorgos–Altynkol: 2	Altynkol inbound: 39.6	Khorgos outbound: 10.9
	Altynkol outbound: n.a.	Khorgos inbound: n.a.
Erenhot–Zamyn Uud: n.a.	Zamyn Uud inbound: 22.9	Erenhot outbound: 11.9
	Zamyn Uud outbound: 11.8	Erenhot inbound: 55.7

n.a. = Not Available.

Though Corridor Performance Measurement and Monitoring (CPMM) records crossings of any type of trains, not only container trains, that may need more time to tranship cargoes from wagon to wagon, the substantial differences in time reflect other inefficiencies such as availability of wagons, waiting at shunting yards, customs and inspections.

Souce: United Transport and Logistics Company and CPMM 2018.

Box 11: Rail Costs: People's Republic of China–Europe against People's Republic of China–Central Asia

Despite lack of transparency, there are indications that rail costs are higher from the People's Republic of China (PRC) to Central Asia countries than to Europe. As can be seen in the table below these differences are higher with shipments to Uzbekistan and Mongolia.

Railway Tariffs on Selected Routes ($/kilometer per forty-foot equivalent unit)

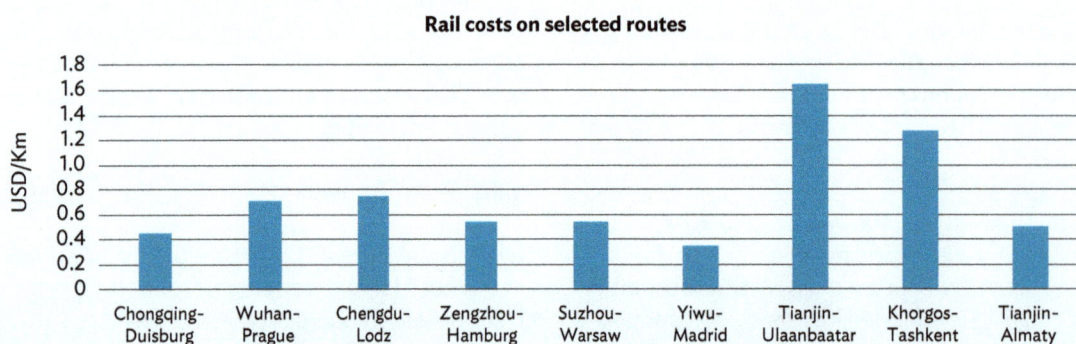

Rail costs on selected routes

These differences could reflect various issues: (i) lack of economies of scale because of lower volumes; (ii) higher railway tariffs by some national railways (this may be the case in Uzbekistan railways); (iii) higher impact of fixed costs (terminal operations, loading, documents, etc.) for shorter routes; and (iv) PRC rail policy to subsidize Europe-bound traffic but less interested in supporting captive traffics to Central Asia.

Sources: EDB 2019; KTZ Express Tariffs 2019; stakeholder interviews.

In practice, most cargoes originated in the PRC reach the western border by rail. Only some local production between the Xinjiang–Uygur Autonomous Region (XUAR) and Central Asian countries move by truck. Despite all countries' adherence to TIR, as a rule of thumb foreign tucks are not moving into the PRC beyond Urumqi or Kashgar, because of regulatory and operational restrictions, thus they need to be cross-docked either in Urumqi, Kashgar, or Khorgos. Neighbor countries apply similar restrictions, e.g., trucks from the PRC not moving beyond Almaty. Private stakeholders complain about waiting times spent at transhipment facilities on the PRC side. Transhipment time at Khorgos or Kashgar is said to take minimum 1 day.

East to west movements are more expensive than west to east as a result of imbalance of flows. However, some sources mention quite expensive costs that may reflect the impact of waiting times and other frictions when origin is within the PRC.

Consulted stakeholders acknowledge improvements regarding crossing borders though some hassle and unofficial payments are still needed to streamline procedures. Despite this positive trend, local issues sometimes flare up as happened at KAZ/KGZ border in 2019.

Many trunk roads serving the PRC–Central Asia corridors have been upgraded, though some issues are to be noted:

(i) Many new sections have dual carriageway and four lanes but not meet proper motorway standards since they are not insulated from surroundings, cross urban settlements and have no a limited number of intersections.

(ii) When new sections are tolled, quite often trucks keep using the old road to avoid payment, even if these alternative crosses urban settlements, adding congestion and increasing risks of accidents.[32]

(iii) Some sections on remote regions and approaching borders still have poor condition and tortuous path, e.g. Osh to Irkeshtam Pass, Torugart pass, Dushanbe to Kulma Pass. Driving heavy trucks on these sections can be highly challenging, especially in winter, reducing the number of operators willing to use it and driving transport costs up. Additionally, BCP facilities in these remote places are often inadequate, insufficiently staffed or have reduced opening times, sometimes not matching opening times at both sides.

Road transport sector in Central Asia complains about competition from Turkish haulage companies. Usually they are moving Turkish exports into Central Asia and can offer attractive discounted rates for their backhaul trips. Though unpopular with local transport companies these bargains benefit some manufacturing and agriculture exports to Turkey and Europe. However, Turkish trucks do not seem to play a substantial role in the increasing flows China-Central Asia-Europe.

Table 8: Road Transport Costs in the People's Republic of China–Central Asia

Route	Fare 40' or 20 Ton load	$/kilometer
Tashkent–Khorgos	1,200	1.04
Khorgos–Tashkent	2,200	1.91
Tashkent–Kashgar	1,100–1,400	1.00–1.27
Almaty–Tashkent	1,500–2,000	1.8–2.5
Khorgos (PRC side)–Kazakhstan	NA	1.42
Kazakhstan–Khorgos (PRC side)	NA	1.29

NA = Not Available, PRC = People's Republic of China.

Sources: Corridor Performance Measurement and Monitoring 2018; Eurasian Development Bank 2019; KTZ Express Tariffs 2019; Georgia Rail Tariffs 2019, United Transport and Logistics Company tariffs 2019, Stakeholder interviews, and www.della.eu.

---

[32] Evidence of this was found during the consultants' field visit, when few trucks were observed using the new toll motorway Almaty–Khorgos while many used the old nontolled road.

5.5.3. Intermodality and Logistics Centers

Intermodal rail terminals in Central Asia are still relatively small in size and throughput compared with benchmarks in Western Europe or other developed countries. Typical throughput for a major intermodal terminal in Tashkent or Almaty is 1–3 trains per day / 20,000/30,000 TEU per year,[33] while typical infrastructure in Western Europe would handle no less than 10 trains per day and 100,000 boxes per year as illustrated in Table 9.

Moreover, most rail terminals in Central Asia have loading and unloading areas shorter than a typical block train that implies costly and time-consuming cutting and shunting operations. Extension is difficult since they are often surrounded by built up areas.

A common feature of today's logistics in Kazakhstan and Uzbekistan is single wagon delivery to manufacturing plants and warehouses. This is a legacy from the time when railways were the default mode of transportation in most of the former Soviet Union. Door-to-door wagon delivery requires costly and time-consuming shunting operations as well as an extensive rail infrastructure such as sidings, spurs, signals, and level crossings that have to be maintained under required operational standards, usually set by the railways authority even if they are privately owned. Shunting staff and locos also need to be available. Risks of damage, derailment, accidents, or delays add complexity. Companies and railways tend to shun away from this complex and costly practice and use trucks for last mile delivery from rail terminals except when sizeable volumes are moved, e.g., car factories, chemical plants, steel mills, grains silos/mills.

The layout of some industrial and logistics areas reflects this practice as branches and spurs penetrate industrial areas and the size and shape of plots accommodate to them. However, modern logistics warehouses have a rectangular shape so that they can maximize the number of loading quays as well as organize their interior with racks, expedition, and reception areas. Legacy industrial layouts are incompatible with the typical grid structure of modern logistics parks.[34]

Almaty and Tashkent, the two main agglomerations and business hubs in Central Asia, have developed some mew logistics parks featuring Class A warehouses, container terminals, and freight centers. Some private sector developments are also appearing in Nur Sultan. Such structured logistics areas are not yet found in Bishkek or Dushanbe. It is likely that private sector will continue to develop new logistics and intermodal projects featuring more efficient and less constrained layouts, including some Class A warehouses. Again Kazakhstan and to lesser extent Uzbekistan are leading this trend in the region, though some studies have alerted about risks of excess of supply as related to the maturity of the market (World Bank 2013).[35]

Table 9: Throughput on a Benchmark of Intermodal Terminals in Europe

	Trains per day	Volumes	Unit
Delta 3 (France)	15	200,000	Movements
Nuremberg (Germany)	NA	480,000	Twenty-foot equivalent unit (TEU)
Ludwigshafen (Germany)	38	300,000	Intermodal Transport Unit (ITU)
Verona (Italy)	38	NA	
Bologna (Italy)	28	NA	
Novara (Italy)	NA	165,000	ITU
Barcelona Port (Spain)	NA	260,000	TEU

Sources: Delta 3. http://www.delta-3.com/; Bayernhafen. https://www.bayernhafen.de/hafen/nuernberg/; Contargo. https://www.contargo.net/en/terminals/ludwigshafen/; Interporto Bologna S.p.A. https://www.interporto.it; Interporto Quadrante Europa. https://www.quadranteeuropa.it/; CIM S.p.A. Interporto di Novara. https://www.cimspa.it/; Port de Barcelona. http://www.portdebarcelona.cat/en.

[33] Sources: Site visits interviews and International Transport Forum 2019.

[34] During the consultants' site visits, rail tracks alongside warehouses in some places seemed to have been idle for a long period. When some activity was reported it was tiny and associated warehouses were underused.

[35] See also: World Bank. 2013. *Improvement and Further Development of Kazakhstan's Logistics System*. Washington, DC.

Container terminal near Almaty 1. Length of loading quay, around 300 meters

Container terminal near Almaty 2. Length of loading quay, around 250 meters

Damu Logistics (Almaty) Length of loading quay, around 400 meters

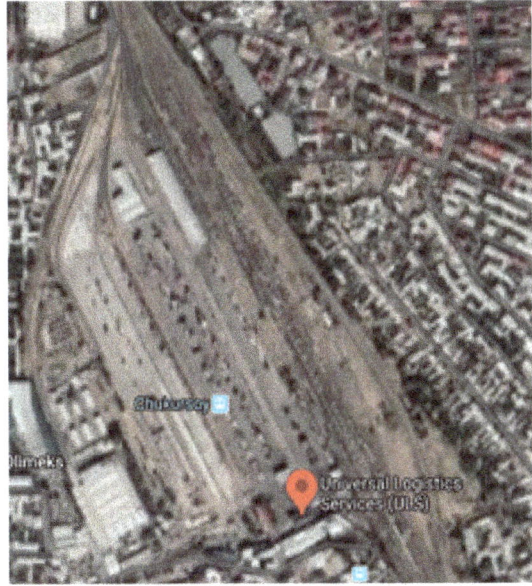

Tashkent ULS Intermodal terminal. Length of loading quay, around 500 meters

Tashkent Sergeli Freight Station. Length of loading quay, around 400 meters

Bishkek Container terminal. Length of loading quay, around 300 meters

Source: Google Maps.

The urban pattern of this industrial area in Tashkent reflects a layout guided by the alignment of rail sidings and spurs.

Source: Google Maps; consultants' team field visits.

Rail sidings along warehouses in a logistics park in Tashkent. Often warehouses are designed with one side for rail and the opposite side for trucks.

Class A warehouse in Tashkent, Kazakhstan.

Figure 20: SWOT: Pacific - Trans-PRC Corridor

Strengths	Weaknesses
1. Well-developed container rail connections.	1. Despite improved infrastructure, still long times required to go through border crossing points.
2. Improved rail border crossing facilities in the People's Republic of China (PRC)/Kazakhstan with possibility of providing further capacity.	2. Infrastructure bottlenecks on roads, in particular on mountain roads connecting the Kyrgyz Republic–the PRC and Tajikistan–the PRC.
3. Relatively good logistics capabilities and infrastructure, especially in Uzbekistan and Kazakhstan.	3. Governance frameworks not always facilitating open, fair, and transparent playing field for the private sector.

Opportunities	Threats
1. Increased openness and cooperation among countries reducing existing barriers for free movements across countries.	1. Focus on the PRC–Europe block trains may impact negatively flows to and from Central Asian countries (capacity shortages, higher transport fares, less priority when allocating rail slots).
2. Incipient development of logistics centers and container facilities featuring international standards.	2. Impact on rail demand when subsidies are cut down or cancelled.
3. Development of rail and road infrastructure from Uzbekistan to the PRC across the Kyrgyz Republic will open a new trade corridor.	

SWOT = Strengths, Weaknesses, Opportunities, and Threats.

Source: Consultants.

5.5.4. SWOT Analysis

Figure 20 in SWOT format summarizes main findings in the Pacific-Trans-PRC corridor.

5.6.   Pacific - Trans–Siberia (CAREC 3, 4)

5.6.1. Rail Transport

Rail access to Central Asia from Russian ports in the far east is assured by the Tran Siberian Line and the Baikal–Amur line. This is robust infrastructure with limited bottlenecks and congestion. The Trans-Siberian corridor is perceived as a more reliable option than PRC to link with the Republic of Korea and Japan.[36]

Russian Railways (RZD) is consistently increasing its container traffic, moving more than 4.4 million containers in 2018, 50% more than in 2012. Container trains in the Russian Federation have more capacity than China Rail's (around 60 FEU per train in the Russian Federation, versus around 40 in the PRC), thus having a competitive advantage. Fares for international rail transport are more transparent and do not seem to be directly subsidized.

As a result of being an integrated network during the former Soviet Union, the Russian Federation and Kazakhstan networks are linked in more than a dozen of places and moving across borders is relatively streamlined by the fact of using the same gauge, OSJD/SMGS standards and EAEU membership. Further crossing form Kazakhstan into Uzbekistan and the Kyrgyz Republic does not pose any technically major challenge though delays caused by lack of equipment, traffic restrictions, scheduling, are mentioned by consulted stakeholders.

The Trans-Siberian corridor is critical for some Central Asia countries, such as Uzbekistan that has intense trade with the Republic of Korea, with volumes up to 2 million tons and $3.2 billion in value.[37] A key driver of volumes is car components supplied from the Republic of Korea bound to the General Motors plant in Asaka in the Fergana valley that produces average 250,000 cars per year. Only this traffic involves about 2,000 container per year equivalent to one block train per week. From 2009 to 2018 Uzbek exports sent through Nakhodka have amounted to 10%–20% of total, mainly grains, grinding products, ferrous metals, and chemical products and fertilizers.

However, due to long distances, transport costs in this corridor are high. Average transport cost per 40' container is around $5,000–$5,200 from the

---

[36] This opinion was voiced by several private sector stakeholders to the consultants during the field visits.

[37] Source: interview with Ministry of Investment and Foreign Trade.

Republic of Korea to Asaka and $4,500–$5,000 to Tashkent (fare includes ferry from the Republic of Korea to Nahodka). This equals to $0.55–$0.6/km for the 8,000+ km overland journey from Nahodka. In comparison fares from Japan or the Republic of Korea ports to Warsaw, Hamburg, or Rotterdam are $4,700–$5,000, representing about $4.3–$4.5/km for a journey of 11,000 km.

There is no gauge change either between the Russian Federation and Mongolia and railways are also governed by OSDJ/SMGS standards. The cargo flow at this border crossing is hugely unbalanced with most of the traffic running in direction from the Russian Federation to Mongolia. An average of 150 wagons per day were received in Mongolia from the Russian Federation. Approximately half of the wagons were Mongolian imports and half of them are transits to PRC. Time to cross the border at Sukhbaatar has improved from about 12 hrs. in 2014 and 2015 to 7.4 hrs. in 2018.[38]

5.6.2. Road

No stakeholder interviewed has mentioned road transport to be used for cargoes to/from the Russian Federation's far east ports into Central Asian countries.

5.6.3. SWOT Analysis

Figure 21 in SWOT format summarizes main findings in the Pacific-Trans-Siberia corridor.

Figure 21: SWOT: Pacific – Trans-Siberia Corridor

Strengths	Weaknesses
1. Robust and reliable rail.	1. Long distances and costs.
2. Seamless rail connectivity (1520 mm, SMGS).	2. Road transport is not a workable option.
Opportunities	Threats
1. Further integration within EAEU further facilitates trade flows.	1. Russian Railways focusing on east–west block train flows and not prioritizing Central Asia smaller markets resulting in higher fares or less priority at scheduling trains.

EAEU = Eurasian Economic Union; SMGS = Agreement on International Railway Freight Communications; SWOT = Strengths, Weaknesses, Opportunities, and Threats.

Source: Consultants.

[38] Source: CPMM 2018.

6. CAREC Plans and Projects in Ports and Logistics

6.1. Introduction

CAREC countries have been active in developing strategies to insert themselves in the global flows of goods, defining their own plans and priorities. A number of international transport corridors have been promoted across CAREC countries both by multinational cooperation frameworks as mentioned in section 4.5 and included into national transport and infrastructure plans. A non-exhaustive list of these is provided as follows:

(i)   Eurasia Land Bridge Economic Corridor (BRI).
(ii)   PRC, Mongolia, Russian Federation Economic Corridor (BRI).
(iii)   PRC–Central Asia, West Asia Economic Corridor (BRI).
(iv)   PRC–Pakistan Economic Corridor (BRI).
(v)   Trans-Caspian International Transport Route (TITR/TMTM).
(vi)   TRACECA Corridor: EU - Turkey / Georgia – Central Asia.
(vii)   Lapis Lazuli Corridor: Afghanistan / Turkmenistan - Azerbaijan - Georgia / Turkey – EU.
(viii) West Route of the North-South Corridor: Russian Federation – Azerbaijan – Iran.
(ix)   East Route of the North-South Corridor: Kazakhstan - Turkmenistan – Iran.
(x)   Ashgabat Agreement: Kazakhstan / Uzbekistan - Turkmenistan - Iran – Oman.
(xi)   Trans-Afghan Transport Corridor: Iran / Pakistan – Afghanistan – Uzbekistan / Tajikistan.

Proposed infrastructure on those corridors aims at improving efficiency in already busy routes or at filling missing links between nodes. However quite often infrastructure projects are conceived from a supply-side approach with the assumption that increased efficiency and performance will trigger volumes and induce economic development, in particular in backward regions. Sometimes these corridors are associated to new developments such as new ports, new urban centralities. Moreover, international infrastructure projects need to be complemented with improving domestic connectivity (ITF 2019).[39]

The consultants have carried out an extensive review of country plans and projects on ports, logistics and related fields for the last 10–15 years. Volume III includes summary of the most relevant of them per country.

6.2. Assessment of Projects Presented at CAREC Transport Sector Cooperation Committee (2014–2019)

CAREC Transport Sector Cooperation Committee (TSCC) provides a platform for presenting and discussing national plans in transport and logistics with representatives from neighboring countries and development partners. The consultants have analyzed country presentations at TSCC from 2014 to 2019 (both years included).

During this period countries presented plans and projects for a combined value of $44.251 billion. More than half were road projects, 38% rail, 7.6% ports, and 3.2% logistics projects.

---

[39] Global value chain and developing feeder industries as natural consequences of investment in transport and logistics is sometimes seen as opportunity, i.e., building or expanding capacity and capabilities in feeding economic sectors such as shipbuilding and locomotive manufacturing. For example, Turkmenbashi Port project includes a shipyard, which could benefit from ongoing investment and could accumulate capacity with fleet expansion programs. Similarly, investment in high speed rail in Uzbekistan is expected to have some spillover effects in locomotive manufacturing.

Table 10: Aggregate Data from Country Plans Transport Sector Cooperation Committee 2014–2019

Mode	$ million	%
Rail	16,912.48	38.22
Road	22,519.91	50.89
Ports	3,374.30	7.63
Logistics	1,444.42	3.26
Total	44,251.11	100.00

Source: Consultants from Country presentations at CAREC Aggregate Data from Country Plans Transport Sector Cooperation Committee 2014–2019. Note: Information comes from the presentations made from countries and no cross-checking of data has been made. The number of projects derives from the presentations and the scope of projects is variable, in some cases major projects e.g., the construction of a new road may appear as a single project, while in other countries a similar project can be sliced into various road sections that appear as stand-alone projects. The maturity of presented projects is also highly variable, sometimes at early feasibility or inception stage, sometimes work in progress. Kilometers are relevant to assess the size of projects in some projects but not in other, e.g., acquisition of rolling stock, IT systems, logistics hubs or ports. Budgets are not always provided and thus appear as "n.a." in some cases. Accuracy in budgets has not been checked and may not coincide with other sources. Information from Turkmenistan and the People's Republic of China has insufficient detail so that aggregate data could be calculated.

Some aggregate data from these plans and projects are shown in the following tables and figures.

Figure 22: Country Comparison Project Costs: Total

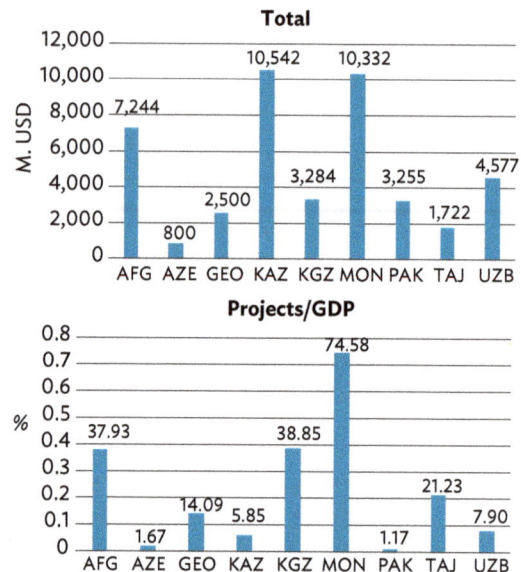

AFG = Afghanistan, AZE = Azerbaijan, GEO = Georgia, KAZ = Kazakhstan, KGZ = Kyrgyz Republic, MON = Mongolia, PAK = Pakistan, TAJ = Tajikistan, UZB = Uzbekistan.

Data from Azerbaijan includes only ports and logistics projects. Data from Georgia includes only ports projects. Data from Tajikistan includes only road and logistics projects.

Source: Consultants from country presentations at CAREC Country Plans Transport Sector Cooperation Committee. Gross domestic product data from World Bank database.

Table 11: Transport Sector Cooperation Committee Plans by Country, 2014–2019

AFGHANISTAN	Number of projects	Km	Project cost ($ million)	% over cost	AZERBAIJAN	Number of projects	Km	Project cost ($ million)	% over cost
Rail	9	2,119.00	4,236.00	58.47	Rail	21	1,553.00	n.a.	n.a.
Road	14	1,488.00	2,408.55	33.25	Roads	5	385.88	n.a.	n.a.
Logistics hubs	6		600.00	8.28	Seaports	1		750.00	n.a.
Total	29	3,607.00	7,244.55	100.00%	Logistics hubs	1		50.00	n.a.
					Total	28	1,938.88	n.a.	n.a.

GEORGIA	Number of projects	Km	Project cost ($ million)	% over cost	KAZAKHSTAN	Number of projects	Km	Project cost ($ million)	% over cost
Rail	7	350.00	n.a	n.a.	Rail	12	4,294.20	2,442.30	23.17
Road	2	630.00	n.a.	n.a.	Road	18	10,608.00	7,944.50	75.36
Seaports	1		2,500.00	n.a.	Seaports	1		124.30	1.18
Logistics hubs	2		n.a.	n.a.	Logistics hubs	1		31.60	0.30
Total	12	980.00	n.a.	n.a.	Total	32	14,902.20	10,542.70	100.00

continued on next page

Table 11 continued

KYRGYZ REPUBLIC					MONGOLIA			
	Number of projects	Km	Project cost ($ million)	% over cost		Number of projects	Km	Project cost ($ million)	% over cost
Rail	4	480.00	334.00	10.17	Rail	12	4,213	5,703	55.20
Road	16	3,090.50	2,927.65	89.13	Road	14	3,476.8	3,888	37.63
Logistics hubs	1		15.00	0.46	Logistics hubs	4		741	7.17
Trade and transport	1		8.00	0.24	**Total**	**30**	**7,689.8**	**10,332**	**100.00**
Total	**22**	**3,570.50**	**3,284.65**	**100.00%**					

PAKISTAN					TAJIKISTAN			
	Number of projects	Km	Project cost ($ million)	% over cost		Number of projects	Km	Project cost ($ million)	% over cost
Rail	1	n.a.	665.00	20.43	Rail	1	55.00	n.a.	n.a.
Road	26	5,947.00	2,590.00	79.57	Road	21	1,596.90	1,716.01	n.a.
Total	**27**	**n.a.**	**3,255.00**	**100.00**	Logistics hubs	2		6.82	n.a.
					Total	**24**	**1,651.90**	**n.a.**	**n.a.**

UZBEKISTAN			
	Number of projects	Km	Project cost ($ million)	% over cost
Rail	13	2,539.50	3,532.18	77.17
Road	7	807.00	1.,045.20	22.83
Logistics hubs	3		n.a.	
Total	**23**	**3,346.50**	**4,577.38**	**100.00**

km = kilometer, n.a. = Not Available.

Source: Consultants from country presentations at CAREC Country Plans Transport Sector Cooperation Committee.

Some observations drawn for the examination of plans and projects presented at TSCC are:

(i) The countries presenting plans and projects with the higher aggregate budget for the 6 considered years are Kazakhstan, Mongolia, and Afghanistan. The two on top are resource-rich and vast countries. By contrast Afghanistan is the poorer country in CAREC and its willingness to present projects may be aimed at attracting the interest of donors.

(ii) When aggregate costs of projects presented in the six considered years are compared with country GDP, the country showing the highest ambitions is Mongolia (projects amount to almost 75% of GDP), followed by the Kyrgyz Republic and Afghanistan, where projects amount around 40% of GDP. It is interesting to note that just one port project in Georgia (Anaklia) represented about 14% of GDP.

(iii) Majority of countries except Afghanistan, Mongolia, and Uzbekistan prioritized investment in roads over rail. In the case of Afghanistan, ambitious rail corridors were presented. In Mongolia the figure is highly impacted by the Southern Mongolia new railways project. In the case of UZB, substantial part of investment relates to electrification and development of (passenger) high speed lines.

(iv) For road projects the higher amounts were presented by Kazakhstan followed by Mongolia, the Kyrgyz Republic, Afghanistan, and Pakistan.

(v) For seaports the highest presented budget comes from Georgia with Anaklia project that was being reconsidered at the time of writing this report.

(vi) For logistics projects, figures from Afghanistan and Mongolia are very high, though in the first case as the projects proposed seem to be at early stage; in the second because in includes the new airport at Ulaanbaatar. From the rest, the highest amount comes from Azerbaijan, followed by Kazakhstan, and the Kyrgyz Republic. It is to be highlighted that no one of the logistics projects proposed is recorded to be completed.

Figure 23: Country Comparison Project Costs: Breakdown Per Mode

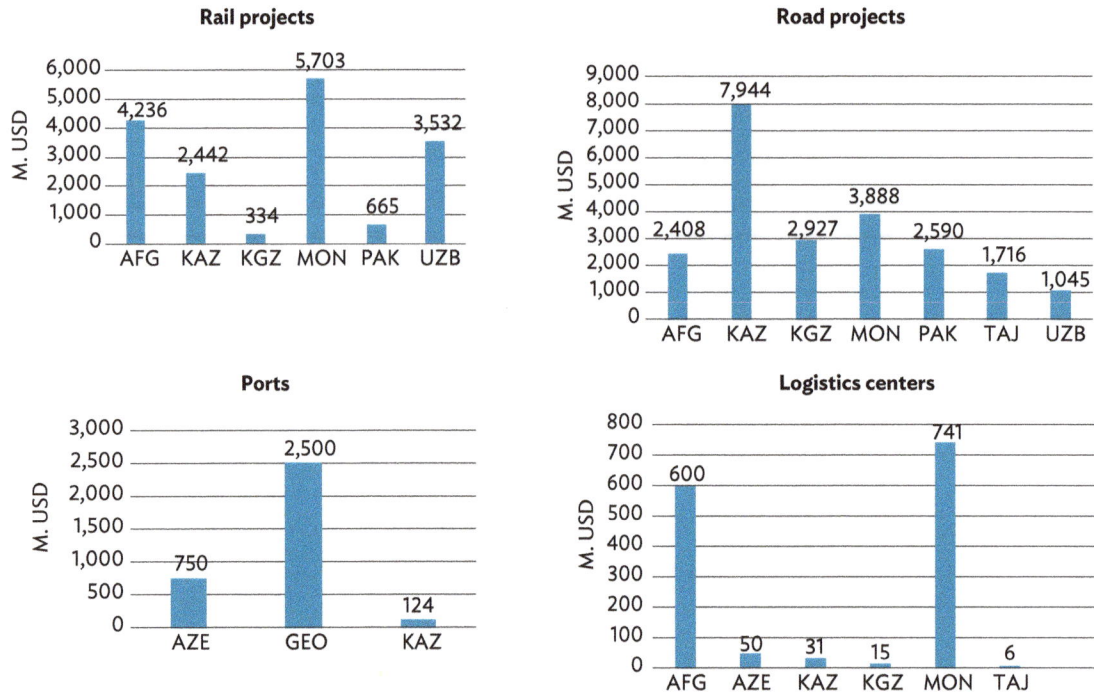

AFG = Afghanistan, AZE = Azerbaijan, GEO = Georgia, KAZ = Kazakhstan, KGZ = Kyrgyz Republic, MON = Mongolia, PAK = Pakistan, TAJ = Tajikistan, UZB = Uzbekistan.

Source: Consultants from country presentations at CAREC Country Plans Transport Sector Cooperation Committee.

This information can be completed with the tables on national plans and projects on ports and logistics included in Volume III of this report. From these tables completion and progress seem to be happening in road and rail projects, but not in logistics center projects.

6.3. Issues in Ports and Logistics Planning and Policy

Some additional qualitative and high-level issues have been identified from the analysis of country plans and projects, added with findings from available literature and discussions with stakeholders from development partners active in the region.

6.3.1. Protection of Internal Markets Drives Transport Policy

Since independence, members of the former Soviet Union have actively focused in developing their national transport systems. Tariff and nontariff barriers, as well a variety of charges have been set up

to protect domestic transport industries and quite often SOEs in railways, shipping, and port industries. Integration of country plans within a broader corridor and regional perspective may fall victim of disagreements, nonshared visions, competition for same markets, interest to protect domestic industries, regional rivalries, and frozen conflicts.

6.3.2. Supply-Side-Driven Projects

Competition among corridors, national ambitions and sometimes a feeling of urgency stemming from rapid growth and optimistic forecasting have resulted in some supply-side driven projects, i.e., supply of ample capacity expected to trigger growth in demand. Projects provide infrastructure now for anticipated future volumes that may take time to materialize.

6.3.3. Insufficient Interaction and Coordination Among Countries

Though program documents and related information on transport policy and infrastructure is usually

Box 12: Caspian Ports

Caspian port expansion projects seem to follow a supply-side strategy and the ambition that capacity will trigger growth for the Trans-Caspian International Transport Route/TMTM Middle Corridor, especially in the container segment.

The new port of Turkmenbashi was inaugurated in 2018 after $1.5 billion investment. The stated container capacity of the port has been set at 400,000 twenty-foot equivalent units (TEUs), with traffic being around 19,000 TEUs in 2019.

The new port in Alat has a declared container capacity of 500,000 TEU at its first phase, while traffic in 2019 was 35,000.

In Kazakhstan, Aktau has capacity for 25,000 TEU and throughput was 14,000, the new Kuryk port has ambitions to offer capacity for 100,000 TEU, while no container operation had started at the beginning of 2020, and the new North Terminal in Aktau has facilities to handle containers, though this traffic was not started either.

For its part Banzar Anzali (Iran) has capacity for 40,000 TEU with throughput being around 3,200 and Astrakhan (Russian Federation) has capacity for 10,000 TEU and traffic around 2,600 TEU.

The typical container vessel in the Caspian has capacity for 225 TEU. At the beginning of 2020 there was only one scheduled weekly roundtrip container service between Alat and Aktau, though port authorities acknowledged that this traffic was increasing quickly, and shipping companies had plans to add some more vessels to this traffic. Container traffic data at ports is consistent with these flows. However, for a port to reach 250,000 TEU throughput (half of Baku capacity on first phase) it would require 1.5 calls per day along the 365 days in the year with vessels loaded 100% and assuming an even import/export split.

Source: Findaport.com, Port of Baku, ASCO, interviews with port authorities during site visits.

available in the public domain, there are few practical mechanisms to allow for preliminary coordination among neighbouring and partner countries.

A related issue is lack of visibility and insufficient factual and reliable information of actual and anticipated bottlenecks, as well as of planned developments in third countries that have important impacts in transport chains to/from far-away ports. Some examples of these sort of issues happening in far-away places are: change of gauge constrains at Belarus–Poland border, developments in ports such as in Bandar Abbas, Istanbul or the Russian Federation's far east, rail congestion across PRC hubs.

Since its start, the CAREC program has played a pivotal role in setting a floor for exchanges and dialogue at regional level, structure a corridor framework, set agreed lists of priorities and align development partners agendas. However, still more cooperation and interaction among CAREC countries is desirable to fully align corridor infrastructure planning and synchronise implementation schedules. The lack of visibility of elements and projects beyond

CAREC perimeter could be mitigated by increased cooperation and partnership with other regional organizations (e.g., the Economic Cooperation Organization or the Shanghai Cooperation Organization, UNESCAP, or UNECE) that bring together CAREC and non-CAREC countries that host relevant ports and serve as transit countries, in particular Iran, the Russian Federation, and Turkey.

6.3.3. Poor Planning Process and Practice

In most CAREC countries, planning process shows poor practices such as:

- **Data availability.** Planning may not always be supported by adequate and reliable data. Improvements may be needed in data collection, updates, and sharing between relevant actors. Data quality and transparency may be insufficient to allow for rigorous and technically sound planning, monitoring, and stakeholder engagement.
- **Quality of planning documents**. Some planning documents have a declarative nature and do not indicate specific implementation schedule, detailed

measures, or the amount and sources of required funding. Appropriate assessment of risks and uncertainties may be missing. Long-term programs sometimes adopted at various intervals and may overlap or duplicate goals, bringing confusing sequences of implementation.

- **Prioritization issues**. It is not always evident that project prioritization is driven by maximization of value for money over other considerations, e.g., political reasons, or appease regional demands for public investment. When these other considerations apply, reasoning to sustain them may be unconvincing.
- **Post evaluation**. Post evaluation (impact/performance assessments) is not always conducted on a systematic basis to provide feedback and may be contaminated by politics.
- **Flaws in stakeholders' consultations and involvement**. Stakeholder consultations and involvement are paramount for balanced economic, social, and environmental impacts and socially accepted plans and projects. The picture in CAREC countries is mixed according to their institutional and political background though generally speaking stakeholders' involvement procedures for plans and projects in most CAREC countries are not always performing according to good practice, nor producing the results they are expected to deliver.
- **Planning and policies reflect the interests of incumbent operators**. Some operators (e.g., railways) may have stronger political clout than government planning and policy units, thus their interests highly influence planning decisions to maintain their dominance in the market.
- **Think big syndrome**. Rapid growth in some Eurasian corridors and competitions between corridors have brought a sense of urgency and to a "think big" mindset. Some other factors are nurturing this mindset such as the availability of funding (and cheap financing) in some resources-rich countries, expectations created by initiatives such as BRI (but not only) and commercial or political interests. However, CAREC countries have extremely imbalanced funding capacity. This syndrome is particularly dangerous in poorer countries share high ambitions with richer ones but lack the resources to implement them.

6.3.4. Inappropriate Skills in Government Planning Offices

Some of the flaws mentioned above are caused by inappropriate skills at government planning offices. Transport and infrastructure planning units are often dominated by an engineering mindset, sometimes derived from central planning times that are still little permeable to other aspects such as environmental and financial sustainability of projects, market analysis, or private sector operational practice. Sometimes operational and maintenance costs of greenfield projects are left out of the equation, or implausible assumptions may be made. Moreover, officials usually have little knowledge about real-life logistics operations.

Officials in some countries have little exposure to international practice. The little they have is from international consultancy and marketing approaches made by construction, engineering or information technology companies with commercial interests. These sources typically focus on success stories but are seldom transparent about failures and risks, not enabling that government officials develop an independent and well-informed opinion.

Development partners and ADB have been active developing knowledge sharing products in a range of issues aimed at CAREC countries. However, there is a gap in knowledge-sharing products in the field of ports and logistics adapted to the specificities of CAREC countries.

6.3.5. Hesitancy and Inconsistency in the Application of Public–Private Partnership and User Pays Mechanisms

Toll road schemes and PPPs have proved to be useful mechanisms to fund capital and maintenance expenditure for the road sector. This is particularly relevant in a region with still poor road infrastructure and insufficient resources allocated to road maintenance. However, it is to be noted that PPPs and tolls[40] need to be considered within a wider range of policy options capable of raising revenue, among them fuel taxes. Hence, road funding shortages in some countries should not lose sight of petrol prices charged to consumers. CAREC countries show a wide range of petrol prices with some oil producing nations

---

[40] PPPs and toll roads are different policy options though sometimes confused as a result of oversimplification. Private sector involvement in roads funding and maintenance is possible without making users pay (e.g., availability concessions, "shadow tolls," etc.). And direct tolls and other charges can be levied by public sector corporations and agencies without any private sector involvement. A wide range of combinations and hybrid systems is found around the world. For more information see: (Ragas, Decision Makers' Guide to Road Tolling in CAREC Countries, 2018).

charging very low prices, while in other countries petrol is rather expensive, taking into account purchasing power parity.

These policy options should be plainly discussed in transport plans and projects leading to a clear and agreed (among all stakeholders) framework for private sector participation in the construction and operations of infrastructure.

Some countries have been hesitant for years to implement toll-road schemes. When toll road schemes are applied, the objectives pursued may not be achieved, e.g., toll roads being underutilized while nontolled alternative ones remain congested. Many countries have opted for levying road charges to foreign vehicles which has become a sort of nontariff barrier.

Private sector participation in the railways sector has been also timid and patchy. While some countries have taken timid steps in opening access to private operators (e.g., Pakistan), in others private ownership of wagons is possible but traction is monopolized by the legacy operator (e.g., Kazakhstan). Institutional and legal frameworks in most CAREC countries are still perceived as frontier markets to catch the attention of international infrastructure operators.

The ports sector should be easier to establish a standard application of PPP, though different interpretations of PPP and circumstances can be found among CAREC countries: from standard landlord ports, to government ownership and management, or even freehold enterprises. However, opportunities for private sector involvement into port modernization may be limited in some cases, as the maintenance and modernization needs are very high (see section 4.2) compared to expected financial gains.

6.3.6. Logistics Projects Not Aligned with Logistics Needs

As seen in the section below even if logistics projects represent a small share of projects presented at CAREC TSCC, few if any seem to have materialized or other type of projects are classified as logistics without really being so (e.g., Ulaanbaatar airport). This may be a symptom that logistics projects are ill-conceived and that planning officials have little familiarity with real life logistics and the needs from operators and international trends in the field.

Some countries have promoted more or less ambitious zones with special status (e.g., free zones, SEZs, etc) offering reduced taxes, streamlined permits, looser regulation, and other advantages with the aim of attracting investment. Some of these zones are in distant or backward regions and often conceived in combination with new transport nodes such as ports or multimodal facilities. The logistics rationale of some of these projects is uncertain. Moreover, governments should be careful that special status zones may be zero-sum games (i.e., attract investment projects that would have been located elsewhere in the country paying full taxes) and be prone to opportunistic companies not setting roots in the country. What most foreign investors appreciate is open, fair, and transparent market conditions; predictable institutions; and reasonably expedited administrative procedures for doing business.

Box 13: Port Planning Issues in some CAREC Countries

Several issues about poor and/or inadequate port planning have been identified in CAREC countries leading in some cases to overcapacity and divergent views on growth and investment initiatives (see also Caspian ports box). Some examples are discussed below.

Georgia

The existing privately (APM Terminals) owned port of Poti has development plans submitted to the Government that would cater for larger vessels and provide increased capacity to handle national freight movements in tandem with the other Georgian port of Batumi. (Ports Europe Feb 2020). Meanwhile a greenfield deep-sea port at Anaklia a mere 28 kilometers (km) north of Poti, has been planned and even a build-operate-transfer (BOT) contract was awarded to a consortium of local and international firms. This new deep-sea port has a design depth of 16 meters allowing for vessels of up to 10,000 twenty-foot equivalent units (TEUs) of capacity to berth at the port. However at the time of writing this report the concession contract had been suspended.

Some authors (Langen 2020) mention that the decision to launch Anaklia project was triggered by historic reluctancy of APM to invest in port enlargement at Poti, benefitting from its almost monopolistic situation in Georgian market.

The situation is that no formal ports master-planning can base the government's decision of either giving green light to Poti expansion, pushing forward Anaklia development again, or both.[1] Thus, the patchwork of situations at Georgia's port sector seems to be a reflect of weak governance and planning mechanisms.

Kazakhstan

Port development in Kazakhstan has included the new port of Kuryk operational since August 2018. This new port development involved the transfer of all Rail-Ferry and Ro/Ro ferry operations from the old port of Aktau to Kuryk port, which is also gearing up to seek new business in the dry bulk, break bulk and container sectors (Gubashov 2020). In addition to Kuryk port carving business away from Aktau, a new port concession saw the Aktau Marine North Terminal open in 2014 operated by a joint venture of private business and state Joint Stock Companies including KAZRAIL (Aktau Marine North Terminal 2020).

The result of these port developments is that currently, four government-owned or sponsored ports operate in Kazakhstan's North-East corner of the Caspian (Port of Aktau, Terminal Bautino, Aktau North Terminal and Kuryk) within a radius of slightly more than 100 km, some of them competing for similar cargoes and most clearly underutilized. The old Aktau port had its volumes reduced in the last 5 years from over 10 million tonnes to less than 3.5 million tonnes per annum in 2019. A national port masterplan would help to alleviate the symptoms of underutilization and manage the retirement of old infrastructure.

A new port concession. Facilities for grains and containers at the Aktau Marine North Terminal.

Source: Consultants Field Trip: Ragas, Sammons, and Khodjaev.

continued on next page

Box 13 continued

Pakistan

Port development in Pakistan had previously been planned on the basis of forecast demand with the construction in 1980 of Muhammed Bin-Qasim port, which was originally designed as a deep-water port to alleviate the land and maritime capacity issues being faced by Karachi port. In 2011 Port Qasim commissioned the DP World QICT container terminal that further expanded Pakistan's container handing capacity to meet growth and demand forecasts.

However, the commissioning in 2017 of the new South Asia Container Terminal (SATC) in Karachi by KPT under private concession to Hutchison Ports added arguably unrequired container handling capacity.

The combined capacity of all terminals in Pakistan is 10.15 million TEU whereas the total throughput in 2018 was only 3.275 million TEU, (WBG 2018). This over capacity for the country in terms of container handling demonstrates a lack of national master planning and lessens the value at the private concessions of DP-World at Bin-Qasim and KICT, PICT, and Hutchison Terminals at Karachi port.

Added to this, the continued development of Gwadar port has been controversial since its inception in 2002. Being far from the hinterland markets of Pakistan and Afghanistan and still missing road/rail connectivity to the north and only single lane road access to the east connecting Karachi some 620 km away. Gwadar port could be regarded as a politically inspired project to attract economic activity to the remote and less developed province of Balochistan, thus development plans include 18,600 hectares of port side land for trade and port services with special economic status. However, the project requires massive investments in landside connectivity to make it a viable future port that adds national and regional benefit.

Port Qasim DP Terminal. Robust and data driven national master-planning of ports and their networks would result in ensuring that ports have adequate capacity at their maritime interface to handle the expected traffic and differing types of cargoes. It would also help to identify the types and expansion needs of landside logistics chains that connect ports to their hinterlands. Different ports face different challenges and national master-planning ensures adequate capacity and reconciling various parties' interests for all ports in the nationwide context.

Source: Stakeholders interviews and other sources cited in the text (photo by Sammons).

Box 14: Azerbaijan M3

Azerbaijan has been busy upgrading its main road axes M1 to the Russian Federation, M2 to Georgia and M3 to Iran to dual carriageway, four lane roads. However only a section of M3 from Salyan to Astara was built following motorway standards, i.e., featuring two separate carriageways, of two lanes and shoulder per each direction, and with separated and controlled access, no crossings or direct access, and with complete separation from any other access by means of lateral fencing.

A strategy on public–private partnership and toll in Azerbaijan road was prepared in 2013 financed by the Asian Development Bank (ADB), which also financed several sections of M3 motorway. One of the strings in ADB loan was that a toll strategy should be applied to ensure the long-term maintenance.

Accordingly, the Law on Automobile Roads was amended so that tolls were possible, but only where an alternative free road was available. This caveat drastically limited the government's options for tolling, since an alternative free road did not exist in most corridors.

Regarding M3, an alternative did exist, the old road. However, the motorway was built according to a prior design that was prepared without being considered as a toll road, especially with regard to the layout and location of entrances and exits to and from other roads. This fact posed many technical constraints to the eventual location and layouts of toll plazas once the motorway was already built. In addition, being designed with many gates linking to other roads, the costs of deploying and operating toll equipment to all gates would be very high.

These issues delayed the opening of the motorway for months once constructed, meaning that traffic had to keep using the old and less direct road. Finally, M3 was opened free of charge for the moment, waiting for a final decision about tolls and tolling systems.

Tolling. M3 motorway in Azerbaijan before the opening.

Source: Ragas.

7. Recommendations for More Efficient and Sustainable Ports and Logistics

From the field visits, meetings and literature review carried out by the consultants' team, some issues have been identified that are hampering or slowing the path of CAREC ports and logistics systems to achieve higher efficiency and align them with international best practice. Based on these issues, a number of recommendations for improvement are listed in this chapter. Some of the issues are not new. They have been the field of CAREC work for a long time and some are already included in the Transport Strategy 2030. Other topics are more specific to ports and multimodal chains and, even if touched in previous or current CAREC work, our understanding is that they merit further attention and could eventually become the field of further CAREC activities.

The proposed recommendations are structured in four pillars: **institutional, infrastructure, operations and capabilities, and skills** and are developed in this chapter. A suggestion for next steps under the CAREC framework for the short-medium term are described briefly in the next chapter.

7.1. Pillar I. Institutional

7.1.1. Open National Transport Markets

Though territories are vast, CAREC national markets are small (except Pakistan). Even the PRC's XUAR and IMAR regions are small markets when compared to the rest of the PRC. Most countries are still protecting their national transport markets and limit the competition from companies and drivers from other countries through quotas. Others are imposing barriers such as visa restrictions, road charges or other statutory hurdles.

Similarly, international railways trips imply costly and time-consuming changes of traction and drivers on borders, even if they make little operational and economic sense. Sometimes the final destination is just a few kilometers away from the border.

Figure 24: Recommendations Framework

Pillar I Institutional	Pillar II Infrastructure	Pillar III Operations	Pillar IV Capabilities and Skills
• Open national transport markets. • Continue efforts to streamline border crossings. • Harmonize standards and regulations. • Improve quality of regulations. • Continue reforming railways.	• Align logistics planning with logistics needs. • Improve port connectivity. • Promote international standards in logistics infrastructure. • Improve knowledge about CAREC freight flows. • Promote good practice in planning including E&S safeguards.	• Promote efficient and competitive intermodal solutions. • Increase predictability and reliability. • Progress towards digitalization and smart ports and logistics. • Promote the Environmental dimension in ports and logistics.	• Strengthen business and professional ecosystems. • Promote qualifications and skills in logistics.

CAREC = Central Asia Regional Economic Cooperation.
Source: Consultants.

Box 15: Fees and Charges to Foreign Trucks

Some examples of a variety of fees and charges are illustrated in the tables below.

Comparison Fees and Charges Levied on Freight Vehicles: Uzbekistan and Turkmenistan ($)

Type of Fees and Charges	Turkmenistan		Uzbekistan	
	Roundtrip	Transit	Roundtrip	Transit
For entry and transit (toll)	150	150	150	150
For transportation of goods to/from third countries	175	0	175	0
For difference in fuel cost	385	86	0	0
For use of automobile bridges	200	100	0	0
For insurance	70	70	5	5
For official services (installing GPS beacon, paperwork, bank interest when making payments)	60	30	0	0
For issuing a Contract for the International Carriage of Goods by Road, route map, and other fees at the border)	120	50	0	0
Total	1,160	486	330	155

Source: Consultants from stakeholders' consultations.

Entry Fees into Uzbekistan for Foreign Trucks ($)

Most Non-Commonwealth of Independent States Countries	400
Kazakhstan	300
Kyrgyz Republic	300
Tajikistan	100 (<10t); 150 (10-20t); 200 (>20t)
Turkmenistan	50 (<10t); 100 (10-20t); 150 (>20t)

Source: Consultants from stakeholders' consultations.

Some opening is being done in the region through bilateral and multilateral agreements. CAREC countries are encouraged to continue liberalization of transport markets striking a balance between protecting national transport industry against dumping competitors and economic efficiency.

7.1.2. Streamline Border Crossings

Though most stakeholders consulted for this study have mentioned recent improvements, delays and hassle are still too common at some CAREC countries' BCPs. Some of the issues identified are:

(i) Electronic data interchange is insufficiently developed.

(ii) Harmonization of documents is incomplete. Translations and language barriers can be an issue on some borders.

(iii) Physical facilities, IT systems, equipment and staff at BCPs are insufficient to accommodate growing traffic.

(iv) Bureaucracy and inertias against change are still prevalent in some customs authorities.

(v) Sometimes customs and other inspection facilities working times are not coordinated with the facility operational hours, which are subservient to the statutory limitations.

(vi) Concerns about security, narcotics, or smuggling along some sensible borders involve thorough, costly and time-consuming inspections. Risk analysis is insufficiently developed.

(vii) Some countries are setting nontariff barriers that involve additional inspections or procedures at borders.

(viii) Insufficient familiarity with TIR procedures makes that TIR trucks are sometimes subject to the same controls than non-TIR vehicles.

More efficient and organized border crossings is possible. The study team has visited very well-organized and efficient BCP sites where a full container train could clear all procedures in few hours. Full implementation of TIR regime at all BCP across the region and provision of electronic pre-declaration (EPD) green lanes which simplifies transit subject to the use of TIR-EPD should be prioritized. Work on trade facilitation across CAREC countries should continue to be a priority as it is reflected in the Transport Strategy 2030.

Box 16: Impact of Borders on Efficient Transport Routing

Tashkent to Samarkand

One example of the practical issues of bilateral cooperation is transit traffic of Uzbekistan's vehicles through the territory of Kazakhstan on the section of the M-39 highway through the Maktaaral district of Kazakhstan between Syrdarya and Jizzakh ("Malik" and "Ok Oltin" customs posts). The opening of a direct road across the territory of Kazakhstan shortened the route from Tashkent to Samarkand, but due to lack of streamlined border crossing point (BCP) procedures for through traffic, the vast majority of drivers still use the much longer route through Gulistan on the M-34 highway.

Islamabad to Almaty across the People's Republic of China

The shortest route from Pakistan to Almaty or Bishkek is through the People's Republic of China (PRC). All countries are TIR signatories. However, apart from crossing two of the most challenging mountain passes in the world (Khunjerab and Torugart), the journey is a major challenge because of the cumulative effect of inspections, delays, destuffing, opening times, change of drivers, etc. that only the bravest entrepreneurs are prepared to accept. One of the few haulage companies operating in this route mentioned the following hurdles as happening at the beginning of 2020:

(i) Sost (Pakistan) border post prepared to process imports from the PRC but not exports from Pakistan.
(ii) Pakistan customs destuff all the contents of the truck in search of narcotics. There are no dogs nor scanners on place.
(iii) BCPs do not open every day.
(iv) At the PRC border post, again full destuffing in search for narcotics, though sniffing dogs are not stationed there but are brought from Kashgar, 300 Km away. Truck remains paralyzed until dogs arrive.
(v) Under bilateral transit agreement, Pakistan drivers are allowed up to Kashgar, where crew needs to be changed.

The 2,000-kilometer journey from Islamabad to Almaty takes about 9 days and costs about $6,000.

Kashgar to Tashkent

The shortest route from Uzbekistan to the PRC is Tashkent–Andijan–Osh–Kashgar. The route is challenging as it crosses three mountain ranges and road conditions may make it impracticable in winter. At the end of 2019 this route was operated only by an Uzbek government owned transport company in joint venture with one from the PRC. Service on this route was launched in 2019 and had made only 200 journeys in 9 months.

The 1,100-kilometer journey typically takes 3–5 days and fares were $1,500 eastbound and $2,500 westbound, but still the joint venture struggled to break even.

Major challenges apart from road and weather conditions were limited capacity at the Kyrgyz Republic and the PRC BCPs, and reduced opening times at PRC BCPs.

Source: Consultants interviews with stakeholders during site visits

7.1.3. Harmonize Standards and Regulations

Logistics flows are facilitated when harmonized standards apply along logistics chains. Harmonized standards also mean that conditions attached to transport and service contracts are equivalent in all jurisdictions crossed by the logistics chain, making markets more transparent and efficient. Some examples of diverse standards and regulations are listed below:

(i)   Though most weight and dimension standards are harmonized within CIS countries, some exceptions still exist as well as other technical barriers and a variety of charges. Compliance and enforcement are variable among countries and even within them. There are not common standards on truck emissions either, nor on driving and rest times.

(ii)   Already some common standards facilitate rail transport, e.g. SMGS consignment note, which works from the PRC to Poland, but it does not work for Turkey or Germany, thus requiring that actors are familiar using joint CIM/SMGS consignment notes. The implementation of the Unified Railway Law promoted by UNECE would be welcome.

(iii) Increasingly, countries are implementing tolls based on different systems. Some require drivers to buy or rent on-board units that can only be used in one country. Other countries require to register and prepay in specific e-toll platforms.

(iv)   Guarantees and advance payments required in international trade need to be done in a variety of systems.

(v)   Not all CAREC countries have adhered to Agreement Concerning the International Carriage of Dangerous Goods by Road (ADR), nor to the International Carriage of Perishable Foodstuffs and on the Special Equipment to be Used for such Carriage (ATP).[41] This is relevant since some key export markets for these countries (e.g., the EU, the Russian Federation, Ukraine, etc.) are signatories. Nor have all countries adhered to CMR harmonization protocol that sets common rules for road transport contracts.

Harmonized standards and regulations would boost regional trade and access to overseas markets. CAREC provides a platform for further exchanges and technical support for harmonization.

7.1.4. Improve Quality of Regulation

Most CAREC countries have taken positive steps to open their economies to private sector and competition. Typically, ports and railways are governed by public sector authorities with various degrees of private sector operations. Though most trucking is privately operated, public sector actors exist in some countries. Regarding warehousing and logistics centers, governments have a major say in planning regulations and access infrastructure, while private sector has the financial muscle and operational know-how.

While regulation is needed it should not be necessarily cumbersome. Regulatory bodies size and scope should be proportionate for the industry they are expected to regulate. Some subsectors (e.g., rail, marine) in some countries are crowded with public sector bodies, agencies, companies, subsidiaries etc. In other countries, however, even basic regulatory system is absent or minimal. Sometimes regulators and operators are not always fully separated. Collusion among some private companies and public sector is happening.

Though improvements are acknowledged, most consulted private sector stakeholders still complain about informal payments required here and there to appease picky officials or streamline procedures. Corruption is favoured by a number of factors: confusing and nontransparent regulations, officials having poor information and training, organized rackets of rent-seeking officials, exploiting foreign drivers' poor language skills and familiarity with the country, among others. Corruption may not only be found in transport and crossing borders. It may also affect planning and permits required to develop infrastructure such as logistics centers and warehouses.

Efficient multimodal chains require an institutional environment setting clear and predictable rules for public and private sectors, and providing a fair level of competition among all involved parties. Exchanges

---

[41] The PRC, Mongolia, Pakistan, Afghanistan, the Kyrgyz Republic, and Turkmenistan had not adhered to ADR at the time of writing this report. The same except the Kyrgyz Republic had not adhered to ATP.

Box 17: Examples of Nonharmonized Standards and Other Barriers

Truck Weights and Dimensions

Under the Minsk Agreement (1999) the maximum weight of a standard combined vehicle of two axle tractor and three axle semitrailer (as shown in figure) is set at 38 tons.

However, Uzbekistan requested some exceptions in the Agreement, among them a maximum weight for a similar composition up to 40 tons, that is also the standard in the European Union (EU), the Russian Federation, and Turkey.

As per other exceptions requested by Kazakhstan, maximum weight for triaxial semi-trailers with double wheels distanced between 1.3 and 1.8 m should not exceed 21.2 tons, while the standard set at the agreement is 22.5 tons. This means that trucks from neighboring countries moving across KAZ cannot be fully loaded. The standard in the EU and Turkey is 24 tons.

For more detailed info see: UNESCAP: *Handbook on Cross-border Transport along the Asian Highway Network*. Bangkok 2017

Environmental Standards

Various environmental standards also apply, either for the selling of vehicles within a country and for the circulation of vehicles.

Environmental Standards for Trucks in Selected Countries

Country	Minimum for Selling	Minimum for Circulation
Azerbaijan	n.a.	Euro III
Georgia	Euro IV	n.a.
Kazakhstan	Euro IV	Euro IV or Euro III + charge
Kyrgyz Republic	Euro II-III	Euro II-III
Tajikistan	Euro II-III	Euro II-III
Uzbekistan	Euro IV from 2020	n.a.

n.a. = not available.

Source: Consultants from stakeholders' consultations.

of best practice in regulatory frameworks could be possible through CAREC network and the support of development partners. Countries and development partners should also intensify their efforts to substantially reduce corruption and expand zero tolerance schemes.

7.1.5. Continue Reforming Railways

Most railways in CAREC countries are in the process of reform but remain state-owned/state-controlled entities. Many stakeholders complain that railways lack reliability and responsiveness and keep tied to legacy practices.

Pakistan and Kazakhstan have tested some limited private sector participation with mixed results so far. Some public sector railways in the region are in the process of transforming themselves into more flexible and commercially oriented entities. In this process, railways are playing different roles not always clearly separated, e.g., regulator, infrastructure owner, provider of traction, owner of rolling stock, broker of door-to-door transport services, operator of logistics facilities such as ports or container terminals, etc. Though reform is welcome it should also ensure open, fair and transparent access of private logistics stakeholders and freight forwarders to rail transport. In a few countries the pace of reform is slow and railways are still perceived by private sector as being too bureaucratic and inflexible to attract other business than their captive markets.

Moreover, in the rail transport market, some tariffs are subsidized while other are not, and more transparency on costs and fares would be welcome. Subsidies may be useful to attract launching customers and build volumes on some corridors. However, it is worth wondering about the long-term financial sustainability of these schemes and the impact on volumes once reduced or terminated.

Railways is one of the pillars of CAREC Transport Sector Strategy 2030 as they are the cornerstone of most Central Asia logistics chains. A suggested additional field for CAREC railways agenda is multimodality as will be further discussed in Pillar III. Operations.

7.2.   Pillar II. Infrastructure

7.2.1. Align Logistics Planning with Logistics Needs

Appropriate logistics planning requires not only critical assessment of costs and benefits, but also understanding logistics flows and the operational and economic rationale underpinning them. As discussed, officials at government planning offices may not have enough familiarity with real-life logistics or be supply-driven schemes. Projects need to be designed in a way that they may be scaled up if demand goes up but may also be reformulated before a full-scale white elephant is built. Projects may be planned in places for a variety of reasons alien to logistics (e.g., geo-political, regional cohesion, land availability, etc.), without proper understanding that logistics infrastructure (ports, terminals, logistics centers, etc.) are not automatic magnets of economic activity but it is the contrary, i.e., logistics business is attracted to places where there is already activity and demand.

Too often city growth and other more profitable land uses such as shopping malls or residential developments occupies well connected tracts of land in the suburbs of cities that could be appropriate for logistics activities. Similar urban dynamics are encroaching seaports and rail infrastructure. Governments should create enabling conditions in land zoning, infrastructure planning, and private sector participation for the development of

upgraded intermodal terminals, logistics facilities and distribution centers around major urban nodes.

Development partners through CAREC could engage in awareness raising, exchange of experiences and other activities aimed at familiarising decision makers and transport planning officials with real-life logistics, best practice, and trends.

Box 18: LOGISMED Regional Initiative

The European Investment Bank together with Middle East Transition Fund launched LOGISMED Regional Initiative in 2008 aimed at increasing awareness and technical capabilities in logistics both in private and public sectors in a number of countries in North Africa and the Middle East.

Among various components of LOGISMED initiative, a practical guide on the design and implementation of logistics centers was published and disseminated though technical workshops. Also, a number of seminars aimed at public sector officials involved in transport and logistics planning were held in all countries involving lecturers, specialists, and private sector practitioners. More than 200 public sector officials in Morocco, Algeria, Tunisia, Egypt, and Jordan took part in these workshops.

LOGISMED also developed a knowledge platform to facilitate the exchange of experience in logistics projects among public sector stakeholders in the beneficiary countries.

Source: Logismed. http://www.logismed.net/.

7.2.2. Improve Port Connectivity

Port connectivity with its hinterland is a cornerstone of its competitiveness. In some CAREC ports, land connectivity faces some major challenges such as:

(i)   Non-optimal rail access to ports. Often it does not exist or is not operational.
(ii)   Limitations of railways to provide adequate rolling-stock and insufficient coordinated effort to create scheduled train services to and from port nodes.
(iii)   Non-optimal systems for trucks queuing and waiting in an organized manner. Restrictions

for truck circulation and poor enforcement of regulations.

(iv)   Encroachment by residential and other urban activities. Other port or city conflicts such as noise, pollution from port activities, industrial hazards, etc.

(v)   Capacity limitations at the port site, creating the need for immediate evacuation of containers to off-dock terminals.

Hurdles in port connectivity are increasing delays and costs for shipments and causing impacts on the cities that host them. In some cases, improved port connectivity could expand the hinterlands the ports are serving.

The CAREC Transport Strategy does not have a ports and maritime dimension so far. Even if only three CAREC countries (Georgia, the PRC, and Pakistan) have seaports, the other three (Azerbaijan, Kazakhstan, and Turkmenistan) have ports on the Caspian Sea. In addition, ports and ferries are found in other places such as on the Amu Darya river across Uzbekistan and Afghanistan. Thus, it is recommended to include ports in CAREC agenda. International ports and shipping organizations such as the International Maritime Organization (IMO) and the European Sea Ports Organization (ESPO) could become partners to support exchanges and knowledge sharing projects.

7.2.3. Promote International Standards in Logistics Infrastructure

Aging infrastructure, legacy design features, and non-optimal equipment has been observed at some ports as illustrated in section 4.2 limiting throughput and the efficiency of port operations. Upgrading port infrastructure to international best practice should be a priority.

Similarly, rail container terminals should have layouts, infrastructure, and equipment for fast and safe handling. Most loading quays length found at terminals is less than 500 m, i.e., a full container train needs to be cut and shunted in and out. Waiting areas and circuits for trucks are not always optimized, sometimes terminals handle both containers and closed wagons at the same time.

For its part, modern logistics activities are increasingly performed in purpose built warehouses that ensure efficient and safe handling of goods, i.e., with multiple elevated docks to unload trailers, ample manoeuvring areas for trucks, storage area capable of accommodating racks for four or more levels of pallets, even surfaces for the safe manoeuvring of forklifts and reinforced enough for resisting heavy loads, sufficient light and ventilation, fire protection and evacuation systems, etc. These warehouses, often labelled as "Class A", are still a novelty in most CAREC countries. An increasingly typical pattern in developed and upper middle-income countries is that Class A warehouses and intermodal rail-to-road terminals are clustered in specialized logistics areas with a variety of names: Logistics Parks, Freight Villages, Interports, Distriports, Logistics Activities Zones. In some countries these specialized parks have been launched by public entities (e.g., port authorities), in other as public–private undertakings, while in other they are fully private initiatives. But even when they are 100% private, they need an enabling environment to align planning, infrastructure, connectivity and services (Ragas, Design and Implementation of Logistics Platforms, 2017).

It is not to say that all logistics activities need state-of-the-art logistics facilities. Smaller operators or those handling low value products will conform with simpler and less expensive facilities. However improved logistics facilities are enablers to more value-added logistics in safer working places. It would be useful that stakeholders both at the private sector and public sector (ports, railways, transport planning ministries and agencies, etc.) could familiarize with the technical, design and operational practice common in countries with better performing logistics systems. CAREC could partner with other organizations to develop knowledge-sharing activities.

Moreover, only a few CAREC member countries are signatories of AGC, AGR, and AGTC conventions setting common standards for road, rail and multimodal infrastructure. It would be advisable that more countries joined and that standards were widely adopted.[42]

---

[42] At the time of completing this report, UNECE was finalizing a handbook for preparation of national master plans for freight transport and logistics.

7.2.4. Improve Knowledge about CAREC Freight Flows

Currently there is no systematic monitoring of freight flows in and out of CAREC countries to and from main ports. Transport and trade national statistics are not compiled systematically at regional level so that a picture of throughput of ports, corridors and logistics nodes emerge.   Thus, the map of logistics flows in CAREC region is unknown.

Not having quantitative data of flows and their historic evolution across the region hinders the identification of bottlenecks and the prioritization of investment in freight transport and logistics projects. Under the umbrella of CAREC transport activities, it would be useful to coordinate the collection and analysis of CAREC countries international trade, identifying volumes, mode of transport, ports of loading and unloading, points of modal shift and major points of consolidation/deconsolidation and distribution.

7.2.5. Promote Good Practice in Planning including Environmental and Social Safeguards

Section 1 has identified some weaknesses and shortcomings in infrastructure planning in CAREC countries. CAREC program already provides a platform for knowledge sharing in several fields. This could be extended into planning ports and logistics infrastructure.

Moreover, a number of international, regional and national agreements and regulations regarding Environmental, social, and gender aspects are relevant to ports and logistics projects. Though environmental and social (E&S) safeguards are the norm in projects financed by international finance institutions, E&S standards should apply also in privately financed projects and those implemented within the scope of bilateral initiatives such as the BRI and other.

7.3.   Pillar III. Operations

7.3.1. Promote Efficient and Competitive Intermodal Solutions

Central Asia is one of the parts of the world where rail freight transport is still the keystone of many logistics chains. This is an inherited advantage when many other places in the world are seeking to increase rail market share with mixed results at best. While further growth for breakbulk and out-of-gauge cargoes may be difficult, container and intermodal cargo still has room for growth. Not only from shifting cargoes from truck to rail, but also because Central Asian economies will diversify, thus trading more value added and industrial products.

However, the current picture for CAREC corridors is mixed. Containerized rail transport traffic is already well developed and increasing in the corridors to and from the PRC, but is still marginal across the Caucasus or along the North-South Arabian Sea corridors.

Most ports in the world are actively promoting sea and/or rail connectivity to move containers fast and efficiently to dry ports and multimodal logistic bases deep into their hinterland. These operations increase transport efficiency, alleviate truck congestion in and around ports, enable a more peaceful coexistence between ports and surrounding cities, and reduce environmental impact.

Use of containers require reliable turnaround times and cheap options for moving and storing empty containers. When this is lacking, additional front-haul fees are charged at imports to compensate the value of the container or the cost of destuffing. In the middle and long-term it would be interesting to explore the possibilities of other types of intermodal traffic, e.g., swap bodies, trailers, or semitrailers using various combined transport options already available. In the studied corridors there are some pairs of origin or destinations (e.g., Black sea to Baku, Karachi to north Pakistan) where intermodal transport is marginal but has potential for further development of rail shuttles.

However, the necessary enabler of intermodal transport is efficient and reliable railways, integrated with other modes of transport such as road and inland waterways. Hence railways reform, as mentioned in Pillar I, is a necessary but not a sufficient condition.

It is to be highlighted that TIR is a global transit system, which is also intermodal.[43] To facilitate and expedite the transport of goods at ports, TIR system needs to be integrated into customs and/or port systems to facilitate the fast release of goods from ports. Not all ports in CAREC region are able to handle cargoes under the TIR system.

---

[43] A pilot was conducted in 2017 from Slovenia to Iran under TIR system including road, sea, and rail. See: https://www.iru.org/resources/newsroom/first-intermodal-tir-operation-containing-rail-maritime-and-road-legs. Also, cooperation among authorities in the port + TIR and TIR IT tools is being tested in Iranian ports with significant reduction in dwell time at ports.

Box 19: Intermodal Transport in Europe and the United States

Intermodal traffic has been the major driver of volumes growth for railways in the European Union (EU) and in the United States (US).

Intermodal or "combined"[a] rail transport is leading growth in Europe's railways. From 2005 to 2016, European railways lost 4.7% of total tonnage and only grew 1.3 in terms of Tn*Km. However, in the same period rail combined transport grew 32.5% (in Tn*Km) and 50.2% in Tons (UIC 2019). Most ports in Europe are busy promoting rail connectivity into their hinterlands.

Development of Intermodal Transport in Europe

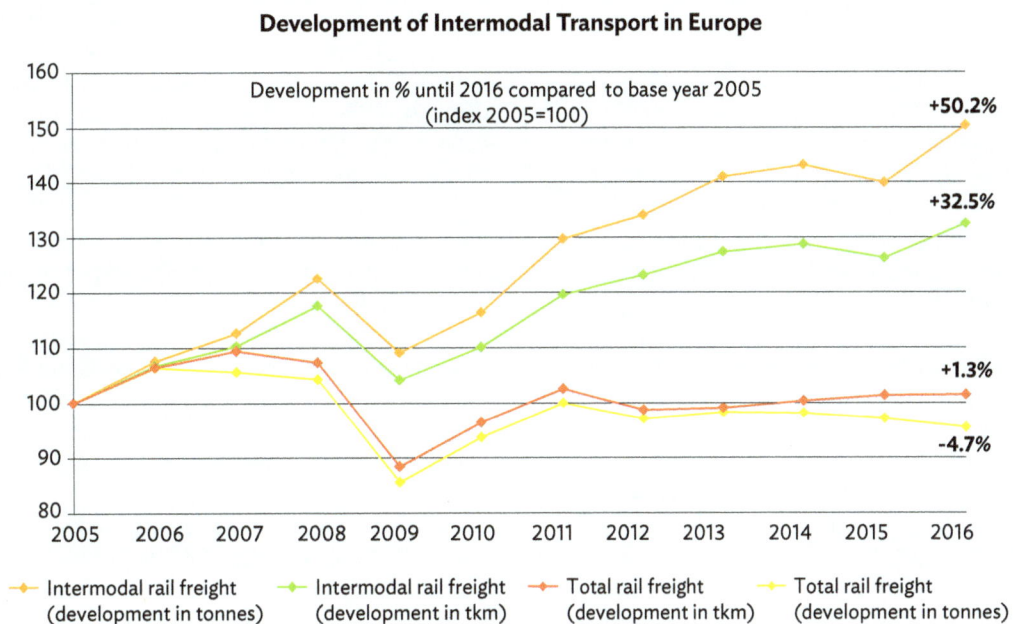

Development in % until 2016 compared to base year 2005
(index 2005=100)

+50.2%
+32.5%
+1.3%
-4.7%

Legend:
- Intermodal rail freight (development in tonnes)
- Intermodal rail freight (development in tkm)
- Total rail freight (development in tkm)
- Total rail freight (development in tonnes)

Source: UIC 2019.

In the US, the volume of containers and trailers moved on railways has more than doubled since 2000, rising from about 6 million annually in 2000 to nearly 13 million in 2013. The pattern of growth was roughly equal to the increase as containerized port traffic.

[a] According the United Nations Economic Commission for Europe, combined transport is intermodal transport where the major part of the journey is by rail, inland waterways or sea and any initial and/or final legs carried out by road are as short as possible. Rail combined transport can use containers (the most common system), swap-bodies, semitrailers of full trailers (often labelled as "rolling motorways").

Sources: US Federal Highway Administration. https://ops.fhwa.dot.gov/publications/fhwahop16057/sec2.htm; United Nations Economic Commission for Europe.

The same could be done for multimodal rail-road transport PRC–Central Asia and Europe

Accordingly, it is recommended that the promotion of intermodality is included as a key issue at CAREC's railway agenda.

7.3.2. Increase Predictability and Reliability

Shippers and importers are prepared to accept long transit times to move cargoes to and from Central Asia countries knowing that distances are vast. But unpredictable times may damage many industries both operationally and financially:

(i)   Factories working with just-in-time supply chains will need to build a buffer inventory of stock available on site to avoid discontinuities.

(ii)   Unpredictability may also spoil exports or imports of perishable produce.

(iii)   It may involve cancellation or penalties on supply contracts.

(iv)   Transport companies may not be able to plan an efficient use of transport equipment. Idle equipment has a cost that will either be passed to customers or erode transport companies' margins.

Concerns about unpredictability have been commonly heard at stakeholders' discussions in the field visits, e.g., (i) delays for delivering cargoes going much beyond the announced times; (ii) schedules being open-ended; (iii) times to cross borders or exit port terminals be longer than expected for unanticipated reasons; (iv) non stipulated delays in obtaining permits or visas, and/or dependent on arbitrary decisions; (v) pilferage of freight; and (vi) weather conditions making travel unpredictable or even impossible.

To make multimodal logistics chains attractive they need to be efficient and reliable. All stakeholders should actively engage in reducing waiting times at modal shift points to the minimum, promote interoperability among their systems and synchronise schedules. This is a field that goes beyond border crossing and that requires cooperation from all concerned parties, i.e. ports, railways, terminals, inland container depots, customs and government agencies and private sector.

7.3.3. Progress Toward Digitalization and Smart Ports and Logistics

Digitalization in multimodal logistics chains could reduce administrative costs, waiting times, increase predictability, legal and regulatory certainty and provide transparency along logistics chains. This involves, among other, extending e-customs procedures at all BCP as well as joining and implementing international standards such as the e-TIR and e-CMR. So far only Tajikistan is signatory of e-CMR convention. For e-TIR pilots have been implemented in Georgia, Azerbaijan, and Kazakhstan, also involving neighboring countries such as Turkey, Iran, and Ukraine. Widespread use of e-TIR across the region is possible since almost all CAREC countries

are equipped with TIR IT tools (TIR-EPD and RTS) and ready to implement it.

Seaports have, in recent years been transforming their traditional approach as infrastructure managers to becoming involved in the exchange of data between the port and their user communities. This transformation has involved development of integrated systems where port and terminal managers exchange information electronically with their partners, using electronic data interchange (EDI), and in recent times implementing port community systems (PCS). Systems development using the internet has allowed ports to provide dynamic real time information that allows port users a communication channel that can be enabled for all participants in the supply chain. Smart Ports is the designation for such facility that includes the Port Community System (PCS) as an open and neutral platform that connects multiple systems, thus enabling the secure and intelligent exchange of information between the different organizations that make up the seaport community. PCS have been developed to allow a strategic alliance between the data they exchange and the single-window concept.

In the CAREC region the seaports are starting to confront the transitional questions of what the port wants to achieve by becoming smart, in other words is a PCS a strategic imperative for CAREC ports. This challenge is amplified by the large variety of service specifics that exists at CAREC ports e.g., pure bulk ports versus rail ferry ports. Defining where the quick wins and long term added value lie must be done in cooperation with the respective port users.

Another challenge is the increased focus on cyber security. Companies active in the ports and logistics industries are responsible not just for customer data (which is already extremely valuable), but for physical goods.

Finally, information and communication technology can substantially improve efficiency, reliability and traceability at warehousing using Warehouse Management Systems (WMS) and at transport and last mile delivery with use of route planning and fleet management systems. Widespread use of route planning and fleet management systems is also regarded as key enablers of more energy efficient and greener transport.

7.3.4. Promote the Environmental Dimension in Ports and Logistics

Transport is one of the major sources of pollutants and a rapidly growing industry at the same time, thus it is increasingly under pressure to deliver environmentally friendly credentials. Increasingly multinational groups or major customers require environmental standards such as ISO 14.001 and associated to their service providers. Other various initiatives such as IMO's Green Ports Initiative and the European EcoPorts[44] are setting standards followed by many ports around the world. For buildings and warehouses, standards such as "Green Building"[45] are increasingly popular and sometimes required by international customers.

Unfortunately transport and logistics in Central Asia is only starting to adopt this approach. Cheap petrol and diesel prices in some oil producing countries are not favoring efficient fuel consumption strategies.[46] Old truck fleet and poor or inexistent enforcement of environmental regulations lead to high fuel consumption. Though rail is more environmentally friendly than trucks it is mostly powered by old diesel locos and diesel back-up generators are commonplace. Only a small fraction of logistics companies in the region, most of them subsidiaries of multinational groups, show any environmental commitment in their operations.

Green logistics is not only a source of additional costs but may also open opportunities for improvement and cost savings. Newer fleet, improvements in aerodynamics or route planning devices may suppose upfront investment, but economize fuel and money in the medium and long term. ISO 14.001 may help companies avoid unnecessary use of resources in their internal operations. Port operations at night are frequently required and the replacement with efficient LED terminal lighting can deliver large savings almost immediately.

Reputation is increasingly an important condition as port and terminal users are more informed and connected with modern codes of practice. In a world with increased environmental awareness, greening logistics becomes more relevant for CAREC countries to intertwine with other markets.

In the field of ports, a number of worldwide developments are identified that could be the field for follow-up work within CAREC program:

(i)   Ports role in blue economy development;
(ii)   Regulation, awareness and investment needs related to implementation of international conventions such as Ballast Water Management Convention;
(iii)   Investment needs/ specific corridors needs on port side (land side) for compliance with IMO's cap on sulphur in marine fuel (investments in fuelling infrastructure);
(iv)   National level policies and enforcement of legislation with regard to air quality as a driver for implementation of shore to ship power (and other solutions for decreasing air emissions at dock);
(v)   Policies and investment needs with regard to climate change adaptation;
(vi)   Investment needs on port side to facilitate IMO strategy on reduction of greenhouse gas emissions from ships,
(vii)   The role of global Maritime Technology Cooperation Centre (MTCCs) in CAREC region in collaboration and outreach activities at regional level, to help countries develop national maritime energy-efficiency policies and measures.

7.4.   Pillar IV. Capabilities and Skills

7.4.1. Strengthen Business and Professional Ecosystems

Improved trade and logistics in CAREC require the emergence of structured business ecosystems at national and regional level, that are still embryonic in most countries. Logistics associations bringing together industry's stakeholders have appeared in countries such as Kazakhstan and Uzbekistan. Even a Central Asia network named LTT has been launched supported by the German Cooperation Agency GIZ. Other efforts to structure a platform of national logistics organizations are under way. These initiatives are mostly welcome and industry stakeholders are

---

[44] See: Green Port. https://www.greenport.com/ and Eco Ports. https://www.ecoports.com/.

[45] See: World Green Building Council. https://www.worldgbc.org/.

[46] In February 2020, a liter of diesel costs $0.35 in Azerbaijan; $0.38 in Turkmenistan; in the range $0.50–$0.60 in Kazakhstan and Uzbekistan; $0.73 in the Russian Federation; $0.82 in Pakistan; $0.93 in Georgia, and only $0.02 in Iran. Source: https://globalpetrolprices.com.

encouraged to keep them active champions for the wide industry modernization.

Currently CAREC Federation of Carrier and Forwarder Associations (CFCFA) mostly includes national road transport associations or freight forwarding organizations. These organizations do not always include logistics providers (2PL, 3PL),[47] nor shippers, merchants, wholesalers, distributors, and many other companies that rely on efficient logistics and supply chains. The participation of entities representing a wider perspective of logistics and supply chains in the CAREC program would enrich discussions and policy formulation. CAREC could also support exchanges at regional and international level among training centers, universities, trainers, trainees, and other involved parties so that they gain exposure to international logistics practice.

7.4.2. Promote Logistics Skills and Qualifications

Shortage of skilled staff in logistics at all levels has been mentioned by many private sector companies as one of the bottlenecks for the industry's development in the region. LPI reflects that most CAREC countries score poorly in logistics competence. The situation is not homogeneous everywhere and at every professional level. Typically, medium to big-sized companies have well-trained and cosmopolitan top management, but standards worsen in medium to small companies and with middle management and operations staff.

In many countries logistics associations have played a substantial role in defining the types of staff and skills required by the Industry, and work together with training institutions at all levels to draft curricula, define, and set target qualifications and skills standards for different professional positions, organize apprenticeship, class-to-work and dual training schemes, etc.

Skills promotion should be aware of reducing gender bias in logistics professions as well as encouraging the access of persons from less advantaged social groups into job opportunities in this industry.

It would be advisable that private sector stakeholders, education and training institutions, and development partners engage in the promotion of logistics skills at all levels, from operational to managerial. Some international organizations such as the European Logistics Association (ELA) or the Association of Supply Chain Management (ASCM) provide knowledge products, training, and certified standards for logistics capabilities at different professional levels. Only a few actors in the region, such as Kazakhstan Logistics Cluster, are starting to be active in these networks.

---

[47] 2PL= logistics providers integrating transport and warehousing; 3PL also integrating value-added activities.

8.   Suggested Next Steps

In this section, some recommended areas for future CAREC work in the field of ports and logistics are suggested. CAREC Transport Strategy 2030 proposed five strategic pillars for regional cooperation, research and action, i.e., (i) Cross-border Transport and Logistics facilitation, (ii) Roads and Road Asset Management, (iii) Road Safety, (iv) Railways, and (v) Aviation.

This report is not going to repeat what is already proposed in CAREC Transport Strategy 2030 but adds complementary actions not explicitly mentioned in the above pillars. These actions are listed below including a short description, rationale, proposed activities, and outcomes:

Action 1: Cooperation partnerships with regional organizations involving non-CAREC transit countries

Description	Strengthen partnership with other regional organizations such as the Economic Cooperation Organization (ECO) and the Shanghai Cooperation Organization (SCO) that bring together CAREC and non-CAREC countries so that enhanced cooperation and visibility of projects and developments in CAREC and non-CAREC countries can be achieved.
Rationale	A significant share of CAREC countries imports and exports are loaded or unloaded in ports and move across non-CAREC countries, significantly Iran, the Russian Federation, and Turkey. These countries are also active members of ECO (Iran and Turkey) and SCO (the Russian Federation but also India, and Belarus as observer). Some exchanges between CAREC with the mentioned organizations already exist but there is opportunity for further development.
Proposed activities	1. Forums for the exchange of factual information and projected developments. 2. Corridor development activities. 3. Corridor performance monitoring. 4. Development of platforms for private sector exchanges.
Envisaged outcomes	1. Increased awareness of challenges and opportunities related to ports and transit in non-CAREC countries. 2. Increased visibility of full multimodal chains from port to final destination (and vice-versa). 3. Synergies with other organizations also active in transport and trade facilitation and corridor development.

Action 2: Knowledge sharing on best practice in ports and logistics infrastructure

Description	Develop a knowledge sharing strategy on best practice in planning, development and managing of ports and logistics infrastructure.
Rationale	This material will provide planners and officials in CAREC countries with detailed information on best practice about planning and development of ports and other logistics infrastructure such as logistics centers, intermodal terminals, dry ports, truck centers, and others, including the environmental dimension.
Proposed activities	This action could include some of all the following activities: 1. A toolkit on planning and development of ports and logistics infrastructure. 2. A web-based resource center. 3. Technical workshops on the issue. 4. Visits to some international best practice projects of similar scale and dynamics.
Envisaged outcomes	1. A knowledge resource to contrast current assumptions with success (and failure) stories in other parts of the world. 2. Enhanced awareness and critical eye by planning officials and decision makers will improve the quality and robustness of studies at the early stages of logistics infrastructure planning. 3. A showcase of development options and good practice in green and smart ports and logistics.

Action 3: Identification of opportunities for multimodal corridors

Description	Identify pairs of origins and destinations suitable for multimodal and/or combined transport.
Rationale	In some corridors the use of containers and intermodal rail–road transport is very low despite distance between origin and destination as well as volumes could sustain rail shuttles taking containers or other intermodal transport units (ITU).
Proposed activities	1. Initial identification of suitable corridors. An indicative list could include: Poti–Baku/Alat, Almaty–Tashkent, Aktau–Almaty, Karachi–Peshawar–Kabul, etc. 2. Identification of barriers that currently prevent more generalized use of intermodal and containerised traffic. 3. Prefeasibility assessments for the corridors with the highest potential and development of road maps for implementation.
Envisaged outcomes	Increased use of containers and multimodal transport on identified corridors with reduced costs including environmental costs.

Action 4: Complement CPMM with multimodal logistics

Description	Review and complement CPMM to include costs, times, and hurdles along port-related logistics corridors.
Rationale	Currently CPMM monitors time, costs, delays, and hurdles found along CAREC corridors but the scope remains constrained within the limits of CAREC countries. Thus, it does not reflect the cost, time, and hurdles encountered to move cargo to and from ports at the end of corridors irrespective if they are in CAREC countries or not.
Proposed activities	Include a sample of multimodal logistics chains linking the most relevant ports serving CAREC in the CPMM studies, assessing costs and times along all the chain. Benchmark against other comparable logistics chains including time and costs.
Envisaged outcomes	1. Enhanced visibility of costs and times (from port dwelling times to final delivery) along the whole corridor 2. Country and regional plans and projects will be better contextualized within broader logistics corridors.

Action 5: Exchanges with national logistics organizations

Description	Develop a program of exchanges between CAREC countries stakeholders with national logistics organizations in other parts of the world.
Rationale	Currently CAREC Federation of Carrier and Forwarder Associations (CFCFA) mostly includes national road transport associations or freight forwarding organizations. These organizations typically invest little attention in wider logistics and supply chain skills, training and standards. However, organizations involving a wider range of stakeholders along the supply chains are emerging in some countries
Proposed activities	A step by step approach is proposed: 1st step. Identify and chart logistics and supply chain organizations within CAREC countries 2nd step. Provide a platform for exchanges, workshops, etc. 3rd step. Put them in contact with foreign counterparts in other regions. 4th step. Work with them to prepare an assessment of logistics skills gaps and a road map to overcome them
Envisaged outcomes	1. CAREC private sector leg enriched with a wider perspective of supply chain and logistics. 2. Soft aspects in logistics skills, training and standards brought into CAREC governments agenda.

Action 6: Country, port, and/or corridor zoom-ins

Description	Country, port, and/or corridor focused reports or "zoom-ins" would provide more focused assessment including throughput, routes, modal split, consolidation and deconsolidation nodes, hinterland structure, market structure, competitive landscape, major players, bottlenecks, institutional aspects, regulations, standards, capabilities, and skills, etc.
Rationale	The recent CAREC work has dedicated limited attention and detail to open-sea ports and transit corridors through CAREC and non-CAREC countries. There is a great deal of literature written and researched that is focused toward the closed networks confined within the CAREC borders and ports but little beyond the CAREC perimeter.
Proposed activities	1. Identify most interesting corridors 2. Identify more interested countries 3. Draft the guidelines and structure of zoom-in reports 4. Test pilot reports for selected countries, ports, and/or corridors 5. Develop a series of zoom-in reports for all the corridors identified in this report.
Envisaged outcomes	1. Useable knowledge and specifics that define and detail the transport networks to and from ports to CAREC hinterlands. 2. Higher visibility of capacity of the networks, present and anticipated bottlenecks, impacts of present or planned developments in non-CAREC countries and costs along the complete transport chains.

www.ingramcontent.com/pod-product-compliance
Lightning Source LLC
Chambersburg PA
CBHW050049220326
41599CB00045B/7336